DIVINE NUMERICS
AND THE
COMING WORLD WAR

MICHAEL DOUGLAS MAGEE, MD

DIVINE NUMERICS
AND THE
COMING WORLD WAR

All Biblical Scriptures in this book are from the English Standard Version (ESV), unless otherwise noted. All images used in this book are from the free public domain, unless otherwise credited. Additional information on this book or related topics may be addressed on a post-book blog site at www.divinenumerics.com.

World Ahead Press is a division of WND Books. The views and opinions expressed in this book are those of the author and do not necessarily reflect the official policy or position or WND Books.

Paperback ISBN: 978-1-944212-14-8
eBook ISBN: 978-1-944212-15-5

Printed in the United States of America
16 17 18 19 20 21 LSI 9 8 7 6 5 4 3 2 1

CONTENTS

Part II How God Uses Numbers In The Bible And In The World Around Us Today

CONTENTS

ACKNOWLEDGMENTS

I would like to thank the many people who have indirectly or directly helped with the completion of this book. These include, although not limited to, Dr. Victoria Sarvadi and our entire Bible study group, Dr. Richard Booker, Dr. John Garr, Dr. Brad Young, Dr. Bron Barkley, Dr. Irvin Baxter and family, Dr. G, Rabbi E., and Dr. W.

Special appreciation goes to those who helped in proofreading the book: Alvin Ocampo, Dianne Beattie, Barry Harrington, and my wife Tawana.

PREFACE

E very war that the United States of America has ever fought has occurred within regular time intervals or seasons. They are NOT random occurrences. Because they are past history, this is an irrefutable fact. The time intervals (in years) between these seasons of war are also Biblically significant numbers. We will be entering the season for WWIII in 2016. In addition, there is another undeniable truth: a multitude of significant Biblically based numerical timelines all converge on the years 2019 to 2020. This book will illustrate these truths and offer some perspectives and interpretations of what might actually happen in the years just ahead.

Many unique and distinctive pieces of information not offered in other publications on Biblical numbers are presented in this book. Foremost is a twelve- to thirteen-year collection of a multitude of unique, unexpected, seemingly orchestrated, personal journeys down numerical pathways that all independently and consistently converge on the years 2019 and 2020. These numerical journeys are presented in an anecdotal format. The numerical observations of data and patterns are truly amazing. Please pay special attention to how the information was received as this elevates the potential validity of the numerical data interpretation.

The most profound chapter of the book describes the probable meaning of two 7s. This most fascinating chapter details how the Lord appears to be using two 7s, in both the Bible and in the world around us today, to numerically communicate to humanity about the timing of World War III and about the greatest event in all of human history, the Lord's return at Armageddon. Two 7s occur in different formats: 7 + 7, 7 x 7, 70 x 7, or simply 77. All formats contribute to a deeper understanding of Biblical Scripture and of potential near-term future world events. The anecdotal story of the 77 Mathematical Equation is also shared in detail. This simple equation reveals connections to the rebirth of the modern nation of Israel and to other important events of the more recent past. It may also shed light on the timing of an important event in the near future.

New terms are presented, such as Divine Numerics and the heart first, brain second mechanism, a mechanism that is in you and is designed by God into every human being. I will also present the scariest number in the Bible. Numerous specific questions on the meaning of Biblical numbers will be addressed, such as, "How can the number 9 be representative of judgment and at the same time be associated with the fruits and gifts of God's Holy Spirit?" This book is full of facts, concepts, and interpretations that you may not yet have been exposed to.

This book should make a substantive contribution to those with open hearts and open minds. It should increase your knowledge about and attention to God's use of numbers in Scripture and His possible application of these numbers in the world we live in today. To this end, I suggest the following:

- Keep it SIMPLE. Learn the BASIC ways God most commonly applies many numbers and numerical patterns. Have a practical and simple working knowledge of how He may be using the numbers so that, for example, when you watch the evening news, you may start to see the potential hand of God numerically marking events or groups.

- Be disciplined to view numbers more from God's perspective. Avoid the pitfalls and harmful delusions of misapplying the significance of numbers to things that are not of God (Please see also Part I, Chapter 3: Divine Numerics versus Numerology).

INTRODUCTION

Numbers are ubiquitous throughout our universe. They can describe different categories or families of unrelated items. Basic counting, size, shape, time, and musical pitch are just a very few. Every day in this modern digital world, we are surrounded by zillions of numbers, if not more. We cannot perceive the numbers of digital coding or of broadcast frequencies. We ignore most of the numbers that *are* available to our perception. Instead, we usually choose to pay attention to numbers that significantly affect us. For example, did you just receive a monthly water bill for $36.26 or one for $3,626? In some cases, we choose to pay attention only to numbers that support narratives or hypotheses that we are in favor of. Politicians, pundits and people loose with the truth frequently serve up biased numbers.

The Bible is also replete with numbers in both the Old and New Testaments (also referred to in this book as the First and Second Testaments). It contains thousands upon thousands of numbers. In the Bible, God may use numbers to simply enumerate or count items or events, or He may use them to illustrate consistency of His purpose and order. But, does God also sometimes use numbers to grab hold of our attention in order to tell us something about the world we live in *today*?

I grew up on the east coast of the United States of America. My family attended a Lutheran church. Because I attended a Lutheran church, I labeled myself a Christian. But I did not fully understand the real and crucial requirements of being a true Christian. Fulfilling the crucial requirement to be a true Christian is not based upon what family you were born into or upon where you attend church. It is based upon what you personally believe and how that belief lines up with the Word of God. My false belief that I was a true Christian lasted until I was 41 years old, when the events of September 11, 2001 (9/11) happened.

Just two and a half years prior to this event, I was blessed to have married my wife, who earlier in her life became a true Christian. During these early years of our marriage, she would continuously place videos of Biblical prophecies in front of me and I would routinely dismiss them.

Growing up, I excelled at academics. I had studied and worked very hard throughout my life. But initially, I had no interest in studying the information in my wife's videos. I didn't need that information. Things were going well. I had successfully obtained my doctorate degree in medicine and had finished my residency at a top national program in anesthesiology. I was in my early years of private practice in Dallas, Texas.

September 11, 2001 changed my life's perspective. Many of the things my wife had showed me in those videos prior to September 11 were coming true! As an anesthesiologist, trained in science and research, this wakeup call of September 11 demanded further investigation. Shortly thereafter, I became reborn in my spirit by accepting the Spirit of the Living God into my heart. I then said, "Lord, what do You want me to do?" and "How can I help?"

After this, I started to receive unusual insights on how God was using numbers. I was always good with numbers and excelled at math and science, but what happened to me was very different from anything I ever had experienced in my life. *This was not normal!* I became unusually aware of how numbers were being used in a consistent manner throughout the entire Bible. The numbers within the text would start to pop out to my attention. And sometimes the numbers would even flash to my attention like neon lights—figuratively, of course. What was going on?

After this started to occur, I began noticing that numbers in the world we live in were consistent with how they were being used in the Bible. I began to write these observations down on pieces of scrap paper and threw these into a big plastic container. The numerical observations kept on coming, more and more. Soon after, the numerical journeys of discovery began. Some of these journeys lasted hours, but others lasted days and even years. What was the purpose? I didn't know at the time. But, it was always a special thrill to be led down a numerical trail to a treasure chest of new numerical revelation. For several years, I just kept collecting the information. Eventually, the big plastic container became totally full.

The Bible teaches that after we are reborn by the Spirit of God, we are given diverse spiritual gifts by the Holy Spirit. Most people who know me in Biblical circles say that I apparently have been given the spiritual gift of being keenly aware of the simple, yet important, ways, in which God uses numbers to talk with His creation. This could be what happened to me. I base this upon the fact that I did not have this awareness before I was reborn in my spirit and upon the fact that this possibility is validated by Scripture. Spiritual gifts are talked about in the following Biblical Scripture.

1 CORINTHIANS 12

Now concerning spiritual gifts, brothers, I do not want you to be uninformed. . . . Now there are varieties of gifts, but the same Spirit; and there are varieties of service, but the same Lord; and there are varieties of activities, but it is the same God who empowers them all in everyone. To each is given the manifestation of the Spirit for the common good.

So, what *might the common good* be in paying attention to how God uses numbers? Is God truly speaking to us through numbers? If so, why would He do this? This book will explore these questions and many others.

Part I, BACKGROUND INFORMATION YOU SHOULD KNOW TO GET THE MOST OUT OF THIS BOOK, will provide a perspective framework essential for the reader to more fully understand the information and messages contained in Parts II through

III. I refer to the study of how God uses numbers as *Divine Numerics.*

Part II, HOW GOD USES NUMBERS IN THE BIBLE AND IN THE WORLD AROUND US TODAY, illustrates the consistency of numerical use throughout the entire Bible. This consistency provides evidence to the current non-believer that the entire Bible is authentic and authored by One God. Thus, information in this book has a potential evangelical use, especially to those people who respond to numbers. I call this group of people "numbers people." For those readers who already are believers in the Bible, understanding how God uses numbers may further strengthen their belief in the God of the Bible and most likely will provide a deeper level understanding of Biblical verses. This can be accomplished by *simply paying attention to the numbers* contained in those verses.

Examples of Biblical verses containing numbers are analyzed in the book. But it is not enough just to understand how God uses numbers in Scripture. Additional fascination is realized when the reader of the Bible lifts his or her head up from reading and sees the same numbers being manifested in the world they live in today! Moreover, one of the best parts about the information shared is that it is not complex! Once the reader is shown how God consistently uses a number, it is easily remembered and easily applied. Part II is *timeless*; having no expiration of its validity. It can serve as a permanent reference for all Bible readers whether or not the events of Part III come to pass or not.

Part III, NUMERICAL CONTRIBUTIONS TO THE Biblical END-TIME PROPHECY PUZZLE, does contain a hypothetical timed model that will be confirmed or refuted by the passage of the next few years. The model contains aspects that are *timed* hypotheses and others that are *non-timed* principles. The timed aspects do have an expiration period to their validity. This expiration period spans from as early as February 2016 for some hypotheses to the absolute latest time, which is 2026 to 2027. However, should the validity of the timed aspects of the model expire, the non-timed principles may continue to be valid and may continue to make a contribution to the understanding of future events.

Biblical end-time prophecy can be viewed as a jigsaw puzzle. Most people in the world love puzzles. Different categories of puzzle pieces exist within the Biblical end-time prophecy puzzle. Included in these are geopolitical pieces, pieces related technological advancements, religious and social trend pieces, and astronomical pieces. The *numerical* puzzle pieces revealed in the book may help link together *other* puzzle piece categories.

PART I

BACKGROUND INFORMATION YOU SHOULD KNOW TO GET THE MOST OUT OF THIS BOOK

CHAPTER 1

WHY WRITE THIS BOOK?

As an anesthesiologist, I have no professional reason to write a book on Biblical numbers. I have no desire for notoriety, nor for any financial gain in this endeavor. I never have written a book, nor was it ever a personal desire of mine to do so prior to obtaining the information I will share with you. But after obtaining this information, I asked myself, "Why am I getting all of this numeric information?" I needed to make sense of this. It didn't seem right for me to keep this information solely for myself and take it to my grave. Was there a broader purpose? I would not have bothered to write this book if I believed the information, as well as the means by which it was obtained, was totally random and had no benefit to others.

I have identified both personal and spiritual motivations to write this book. My personal motivation is simply to help other people who will listen. I remember two stories in which members of my family made efforts to help others that may have inspired me also to help others by writing this book.

One family story was about my great-great-grandfather Joseph H. Diss Debar. He was one of the founding fathers of the State of West Virginia and the artist that designed the State Seal of West Virginia, which is still in use today. He had a history of trying to help others. This can be seen in the book he published in 1870 (with his own money from my understanding), entitled *THE WEST VIRGINIA HAND-BOOK AND IMMIGRANT'S GUIDE.* Its stated purpose was to

provide unvarnished facts and figures to potential immigrants from other states and countries. He described his hope for his book in its preface. He wrote, "It is hoped that its [the content of his book] freedom from all romance and exaggeration may secure for it the attention and confidence of the class of honest and enterprising workers in both hemispheres, whom we are most anxious to welcome as permanent settlers to our infant State." Considering today's debate over immigration policy it's interesting to note that in the 1870s, the focus was to attract honest and enterprising workers. I found my great-great-grandfather's purpose for writing his book to be a noble one. I hope this book also turns out to be a noble endeavor as well.

The other family story that may have inspired me is how my father tried to help out motorists on an extremely dense foggy day in Pittsburgh, PA in the late 1950s. There was a multi-car pile-up developing off of McKnight Road. My father ran down the hill from our house to the side of the road. He waved his arms with lighted flares above his head, desperately trying to warn the oncoming motorists about the collisions that had occurred ahead on the road. To his horror, many people just ignored him and sped by at full speed. He then heard these cars slam on their brakes and collide, one after the other, into the multi-car pile-up. As an analogy to this story, I see many people in this world speeding through a dense fog of deception and heading into collision in our not too distant future. It is my sincere desire that the information in this book may act as a warning flare to the dangers that lay in our future.

I hope to use this book also as *an aid* to reach out to many of my friends who are dear to my heart and who are sorely lacking in critical knowledge and awareness about Biblical implications of what is going on in the world today. What the Bible foretold thousands of years ago has come true in the past, is coming true in the present, and will come true in the future.

My spiritual motivation to write this book stems from the prospect that I may have been given the assignment to do so by God's grace. God has a purpose for everyone's life: this may be part of mine.

CHAPTER 2

WHY SHOULD YOU PAY ATTENTION TO THE NUMBERS IN THE BIBLE?

The very short answer to this question is that numbers are much more important than you might think they are. The Bible contains thousands of numbers. It even contains an entire book entitled, "Numbers." The Bible was written over a period of 1,400 to 1,800 years. Despite this long time frame, there is a remarkable consistency in how numbers are used. This consistency provides evidence that the Bible is authentic and authored by One God.

Divine Numerics And The Coming World War © is written for several reading audiences. These include believers in the Bible, current non-believers in the Bible, as well as to a much smaller group of individuals in the world who can be described as "numbers people."

Who are *"numbers people"*? I describe numbers people as those individuals who have a special affinity for numbers. They pay attention to numbers. They analyze them. They often say that they do not like to make decisions until they have had an opportunity to "run the numbers".

To those readers who already are currently *non-believers* in the Bible and who are also numbers people, please know that God is giving out invitations to all groups of people in different ways. There are many different groups of people in this world. Each group is given a type of information that they might respond to. Not everyone responds to numbers. But for you as a numbers person, your invitation may come to you by way of His use of numbers. This is why it might be important for you to pay attention to the numbers in the Bible.

To those readers who are already believers in the Bible, paying attention to how God is using numbers may further strengthen your belief and provide you with a deeper level understanding of Biblical verses that contain numbers. Most people who read Scripture just gloss right over the numbers. Don't do that. You're missing out on some potential important information and cool stuff. Numbers can add significant depth of insight to the Biblical text.

All readers should pay attention to the numbers in the Bible because they seem to be telling us about major events that may occur in our future.

CHAPTER 3

DIVINE NUMERICS VERSUS NUMEROLOGY

When I tell people that I am writing a book about numbers in the Bible, they most often respond by saying, "Oh, you're writing a book on *numerology!*" I never felt that numerology was a fully accurate term. Therefore, I decided to define the term "Divine Numerics" in an effort to make an important distinction between numerology and how numbers in the Bible are used. There is a natural tendency for people to assign inherent power to numbers. The Free Dictionary defines numerology as, "The study of the occult meanings of numbers and their supposed influence on human life." *Numbers have no inherent power.*

FOCUS, FOCUS, FOCUS on *Who* is the POWER *behind* the numbers!

There is a famous apocryphal story associated with the bank robber *Willie Sutton.*

Question: Why rob banks?
Answer: Because that's where the money is!

I offer an analogy to this.

Question: Why focus on how God uses numbers?
Answer: Because that's where the POWER is!

The power behind numbers is *the power of the one who is using the numbers*. If you live at 666 Ohno Street, don't worry. It doesn't matter! If I do something in the form of a 7, it has little effect upon you. But if an omnipotent God does something using a 7, it can affect the entire world.

Therefore, I will use the term *Divine Numerics* in this book as a distinction from numerology to encourage all readers to avoid the pitfalls of numerology and to focus on how God is using numbers, because when God uses numbers, there is great power behind them. And when God uses numbers, it could greatly affect you.

CHAPTER 4

OTHER TERMINOLOGY USED
IN THIS BOOK

Instead of using the terms *Old Testament* and *New Testament*, I believe it more precise to use terms *First Testament* and *Second Testament*, respectively. This is not an original idea of mine, but I fully embrace the idea for the following reasons.

When the writings of the Second Testament were compiled in the 300s AD, a time or temporal distinction of old and new seemed more valid. But today, I would consider the Second Testament temporally old and the First Testament *older*! With modern English, in addition, one of the connotations of old is no longer valid; replaced by the new. This is not an accurate description of the Bible. The First Testament is still today as equally valid as is the Second Testament. This equal validity is described eloquently yet in easy to understand terms by Dr. Richard Booker in his book, *Torah: Law or Grace?*[1] Whereas, Yeshua (Jesus) did bring us a new covenant, He in no way invalidated the First Testament. Some have described the First Testament as Yeshua concealed and the Second Testament as Yeshua revealed. This describes a *continuation of validity*.

God does things with purpose. We may not understand immediately why He does some things as the Biblical history of the Israelites illustrates. It is common not to understand, especially at first, the ways of God. This is another reason why we need to *trust* in God. "In God We Trust" should not be some meaningless slogan on our American money. God's ways and thoughts are higher than those of humanity's.

ISAIAH 55:8–9

For my thoughts are not your thoughts, neither are your ways my ways, declares the LORD.
For as the heavens are higher than the earth, so are *my ways higher than your ways and my thoughts than your thoughts.* [Italics added]

Even though the Israelites may not have understood the following at the time, is it possible that God had several purposes in mind when He first gave Moses the Ten Commandments written on *two* tablets? Why didn't God use a *smaller font* and put the Ten Commandments on *one* tablet? Is it possible that He chose *two* tablets to tell you something today? His choice was purposeful and not random! It is very possible that God used two tablets to write the Ten Commandments, in part, to foreshadow the eventual compilation of the First and Second Testaments. And Moses broke the first pair of tablets in response to the Israelites rejection of God. So a second pair of tablets was then made. Likewise, Yeshua was rejected by the world the first time and His second arrival to our earth realm is the next order. You may disagree with this interpretation. Perhaps, one day, we will be able to ask Him specifically about why He didn't use a smaller font.

Image of Moses holding *two tablets* of the Ten Commandments

Regardless of whether you agree with my interpretation of why God may have chosen to write the Ten Commandments on two tablets, it is still more accurate to use the terms First and Second Testaments instead of Old and New Testaments. This is even more appropriate in this book; a book that attempts to focus on how God uses numbers.

Finally, here is another term that will be used in this book. I will use the name *Yeshua* to refer to *Jesus*. Jesus is a Greek name. Yeshua is His Hebraic name. Yeshua wasn't born as a Greek. He was born as a Jew. Yeshua means "salvation." His disciples probably never called Him "Jesus" face to face. They probably also never called Him Jesus with a Spanish pronunciation. They most likely called Him, "Yeshua." So, from here forward, I have elected to use the name Yeshua.

CHAPTER 5

WHY YOU MUST OPEN YOUR HEART TO RECEIVE FULL UNDERSTANDING

God designed a multitude of mechanisms inside human beings. One I see frequently in my anesthesiology profession is a *vagal reaction.* This common physiological mechanism explains why people faint when they see blood or have an IV started. I also see this mechanism in play when patients undergo a colonoscopy. In this procedure, a stretch of the colon can send a signal up a branch of the vagus nerve to the brain and then back down another branch of the vagus nerve to the heart. This can result in severe slowing of the heart rate; sometimes on the border of asystole or complete stoppage of the heart. It's just one of many physiological mechanisms that God built into us.

Another mechanism, which is built into all humans, controls whether a person can perceive and comprehend information coming from the spirit realm. This mechanism is every bit as real as the vagal mechanism described above, and it is the way God designed you. And God designed you this way for a very important purpose: In order for your brain to understand spiritual information, this information must first pass through your spirit. Your spirit is also commonly referred to as your spiritual heart. Your spiritual heart is the *gateway* for spiritual information to enter into your body. Your brain then has access to this information. I call this mechanism the *heart first, brain second mechanism.* You must have a desire to open your heart to God in order for your brain to understand spiritual knowledge and wisdom.

The existence of this mechanism is operative in the world today. It is a major reason why it's common to see two or more different people of great intelligence looking at the very same situation and yet see the situation from totally different perspectives. Having a different perspective about a moral situation most often is not about intellectual capacity or about having different past experiences. With the ever-increasing percentage of non-Bible-believing electorate, the existence of this mechanism is also the core reason behind the ever-increasing divisiveness of most political and cultural groups in America and in other parts of the world today. The existence of this mechanism is also why people *change* and see a different perspective *only after* they have opened up their heart to God.

This change of perspective is described in the "Was blind, but now I see" part of the lyrics of Amazing Grace.

> Amazing Grace, how sweet the sound,
> That saved a wretch like me.
> I once was lost but now am found,
> **Was blind, but now, I see.**

God designed the heart first, brain second mechanism in you for a reason. And you really need to understand this. This is extremely underappreciated in our materialistic world. *God cares much more about your heart than He does about your intellect.* Comparatively speaking, human intellect is infinitesimally small compared to God's intellect. Why does He need your intellect? If He was more concerned about your intellect, would only intelligent people be able to get into heaven? This would make no sense and is contrary to the teachings of the Bible. Therefore, it is easy to understand why God would design a mechanism inside all human beings of heart first, brain second.

The Bible clearly illustrates the existence of the *heart first, brain second mechanism* that God designed into humans. Here are some examples.

Yeshua often taught in parables. When He spoke in parables, not everyone who physically heard Him with their ears understood His message. His own disciples were bewildered as to why He preferred to speak in parables rather that language that all who heard could also clearly understand. Yeshua spoke in parables so that only those whose *hearts were open* would be able to receive the understanding with their intellect.

MATTHEW 13:10–15
THE PURPOSE OF THE PARABLES
Then the disciples came and said to him, "Why do you speak to them in parables?" And he answered them, "To you it has been given to

know the secrets of the kingdom of heaven, but to them it has not been given . . . . This is why I speak to them in parables, because seeing they do not see, and hearing they do not hear, nor do they understand. Indeed, in their case the prophecy of **Isaiah** is fulfilled that says:

""""You will indeed hear but never understand, and you will indeed see but never perceive."
For this people's *heart* has grown dull, and with their ears they can barely hear, and their eyes they have closed, lest they should see with their eyes and hear with their ears *and understand with their heart* and turn, and I would heal them.'
[Bold type and Italics added]

Many of the proverbs in the Bible describe the spiritual wisdom of God. The wisdom of God is far superior and more desirable than the wisdom of man.

When it comes to understanding the spiritual wisdom of God, Proverbs 2 clearly illustrates the *heart first, brain second mechanism*. The wisdom of God *enters* your heart.

PROVERBS 2:10–11
For *wisdom will come into your heart*, and knowledge will be pleasant to your soul; discretion will watch over you,

understanding will guard you,
[Bold type and Italics added]

From Proverbs 18, we see that it's the heart that acquires spiritual knowledge.

PROVERBS 18:15 (NKJV)
The heart of the prudent acquires knowledge

Proverbs 3 also illustrates this mechanism and differentiates the brain and heart.

PROVERBS 3:1, 5 (NKJV)
My son, do not *forget* my law, But let your ***heart*** keep my commands; . . .
Trust in the LORD with all your ***heart***, and lean not on your own **understanding**;
[Bold type and Italics added]

In verse 1 of this proverb, it is quite possible that the son remembers the commands in his brain, but just doesn't feel like following them in his heart. Verse 5 illustrates that God emphasizes that you should rely on your heart to trust Him over your brain to understand Him in all of His ways.

Bible verses found in 1 Corinthians 2 also clearly illustrate the *heart first, brain second mechanism.* But it even goes further in stating that it is ***impossible*** for humans to understand the spiritual wisdom and knowledge of God without a heart that is open to His

Spirit. The natural man is one who has not opened up his or her heart to the Spirit of God. Therefore, the brain of the natural man cannot in any way understand the spiritual wisdom and knowledge given by God.

1 CORINTHIANS 2:10, 14 (NKJV)
These things God has revealed to us through the Spirit. . . . But the natural man does not receive the things of the Spirit of God, for *they are foolishness to him; nor can he know them, because they are spiritually discerned.* [Italics added]

This can't be much clearer.

The depravity of man is a condition of *the heart.* British journalist Malcolm Muggeridge once wrote, "The depravity of man is at once the most empirically verifiable reality but at the same time the most intellectually resisted fact."[2]

God never has ceased to interact with His creation. You may not currently see His active hand working today in the world. But if you actively seek Him with all your heart, He will manifest His reality to you in ways of *His choosing.* At the same time, He will remain hidden to those who make an active choice not to seek Him with an open heart. Their brains will never receive spiritual wisdom and knowledge of God, regardless of how intelligent they are.

Even if you are in covenant relationship with God, God will still *test your heart.* Testing will expose the strength of your commitment to Him.

DEUTERONOMY 8:2

And you shall remember the whole way that the
LORD your God has led you these forty years in
the wilderness, that he might humble you, *testing
you to know what was in your heart*, whether you
would keep his commandments or not.
[Italics added]

If you do not understand that the *heart first, brain
second mechanism* exists in you, then you are at a major
disadvantage in understanding the reality you live in.
This is true whether you want to accept this assertion
or not. And this is true regardless of how intellectual
you think you are. In fact, relying on your brains, while
excluding God from your heart, will lead to very bad
outcomes for you in the future. The understanding of
spiritual matters cannot get to your brain without going
first through an open heart. By God's design, this is the
way it works.

So, please remember this key concept: God cares
more about your heart then He does about your
intellect. It doesn't take great intellect to understand
this. It takes an open heart.

Is it time for you to open your heart fully to Him?

CHAPTER 6

METHOLOGY USED TO OBTAIN THE NUMERICAL INFORMATION

After my September 11, 2001 wakeup call, when I started to become aware of how numbers were used in the Bible, I made a deliberate decision at that time *not* to look at other books or sources on the same subject. I wanted my numerical observations to be free from bias. As such, the large majority of numerical information contained in this book was obtained on a personal basis.

More recently, however, I have been asked by others who know of my interest in Biblical numbers, to give my perspective about other works on Biblical numbers. Because of these requests, I have looked at a few other works. I will share some *generalized* perspectives about a few other sources in the next chapter.

In addition, I spent little effort and time getting the numerical information. I actually consider this as something positive; one that increases the potential validity of the numerical information I share. When you consider the numerical interpretations herein, you may at first think that I spent great time, effort, and research in obtaining the information and figuring out the numerical patterns. But this is not the way it happened. I just went about living my daily life and the information was just put in front of my path and I noticed them. Time and time again, these numbers seemed to be orchestrated in front of me. *HOW* the numerical information was obtained is probably more important than potential conclusions drawn from the actual data alone. If I did not actively work to seek out information on numbers in the Bible, then why were they seemingly orchestrated in front of me as I went about my daily personal business?

CHAPTER 7

HOW THIS BOOK MAY DIFFER FROM OTHERS WORKS ON BIBLICAL NUMBERS

This book is certainly not a complete and exhaustive work on the topic on Biblical numbers, but rather special insights that I have discovered in step-by-step increments. You may also find that the interpretations of numbers found herein differ from other sources.

When I finally did look at some other works on Biblical numbers, especially those works related to Biblical prophecy, I found some of them to be overly complex. They left me with an impression that they were more works of man than inspired insights of prophecy. It was easy to get lost in the numbers.

On the other end of the spectrum, when I looked at some other works on Biblical numbers, I found them to be far too simplistic and without substantial validation, especially when simple numerical calculations were used as a sole basis for making major assertions about the future.

In my opinion, one example of simplistic calculations based upon arbitrary unconfirmed assumptions is the

2011 rapture predictions of the late Harold Camping, an American Christian radio broadcaster, author and evangelist. Before his predictions were proven erroneous, I looked into his calculations. Based on those calculations alone and not upon any pre-existing beliefs about a rapture, I concluded nothing was going to happen in line with what he was asserting.

Let me make this very clear. And I will repeat this several times in this book for emphasis. I do not know the future. No human knows the future with 100 percent certainty. No human can validly claim they know the future and the answers of future prophecies with 100 percent certainty. Only God knows the future with 100 percent certainty. With respect to the hypothetical speculative model presented later in this book, if some of the major numerical interpretations about the future found in this book turn out to be correct, I take zero credit. I am not smart enough to have figured these things out. In this scenario, I would just be one of many messengers.

We will be entering the season for World War III in 2016 and there is a major Biblically based numerical convergence on the years 2019 to 2020. I am sharing this information with you, and I am not date-setting. This information *suggests* a time window of immense importance. If it turns out to be wrong, it does not impugn the integrity of the Bible. I am just laying out the numerical data and the way it was obtained *for your consideration*. Together, as we move into the future, we will see either confirmations or refutations of this information.

In contrast to overly complex works on Biblical numbers or simplistic predictions based upon arbitrary assumptions, I have come to the conclusion based on my personal experience that if God wants us to know something related to how He is using numbers, He is going to make it *easy* for us to know. He will also provide substantial evidence to validate numerical conclusions. It should not be difficult like rocket science or mathematical physics.

CHAPTER 8

DO PEOPLE IN THIS WORLD LIVE IN A FOUR-DIMENSIONAL BUBBLE?

Humans live in a four-dimensional material world, three spatial and one time. Specifically, the three spatial dimensions are height, width, and depth. The fourth dimension is time. I dare to say that most people don't think much beyond their four-dimensional reality. They are living in a four-dimensional bubble. The key characteristic of being in a reality bubble is that most people do not know they are in a given bubble until that bubble bursts. In the stock market, the internet bubble and housing subprime bubble are recent examples. Just because one cannot perceive something with their physical senses doesn't mean it doesn't exist.

Take atoms and electrons as an example. Just because we can't see them with our naked eyes doesn't mean they don't exist. I remember studying for an Analytical Chemistry class final in college. I was going into the final with a *B* average, which was not the norm for me; I normally received all *A*'s. While studying, I was having difficulty absorbing the theoretical information I was reading in the textbook. It didn't represent reality to me until I stopped thinking in the theoretic, pounded the study tabletop I was sitting at with my fist, and, in my mind, transferred the theoretic into reality by saying, "In this table, there are atoms and electrons. They really do exist and when an electron jumps from one valence to another, a quantum of energy is released or consumed!" This approach made all the difference in mastering the material for the final. I went home during the Christmas break not knowing for sure how I did on the test. But the report card arrived in the mail and I received all *A*'s for that semester, which included an *A* in Analytical Chemistry.

On the very first day in the next semester's Chemistry class, the same professor began the class by sitting on his desk, swinging his feet back and forth and looking at me for several minutes while remaining silent. When the chatter of the returning classmates quelled, the professor broke his silence and said, "You know, Magee. You did better on that final than I did!" Out of a possible 250 points, I had scored 246. My point is that, just as it was helpful for me to fully embrace the reality of atoms and electrons in my analytical chemistry class, it should be really helpful for you to understand the reality of *all the dimensions* around us.

There are at least six *other* dimensions, in addition to the four dimensions we perceive in our material world. What we commonly refer to as the spiritual world exists within these six other dimensional realities.

2 CORINTHIANS 4:18 (NKJV)

While we look not at the things which are seen, but at the things which are not seen: for the things which are seen are temporal; but the things which are not seen are eternal.

Particle physicists have concluded that 10 to 11 dimensions exist, not just the four dimensions that we can perceive. This is reality. Therefore, please don't' get stuck in a 4 dimensional mindset. This gives a different perspective twist to thinking outside of the box: Think outside of the 4-D box that we can physically perceive.

Dr. Chuck Missler, a former computer and aerospace engineer and now Biblical teacher points out that,

> "Nachmonides was a 12th century Jewish scholar, who concluded, based on a detailed study of Genesis, that there are 10 dimensions in the world that we live, and only 4 are "knowable" (Commentary on Genesis, 1263). Particle physicists of the 20th century (ie, hundreds of years of research and billions of dollars later) came to the same conclusion: The world we live in has 10 dimensions, and 4 are directly measurable (3 spatial + time). The other 6 are "curled" into less than 10^{-33} cm and thus inferable only by indirect means." [3]

An excellent description of our multi-dimensional universe, including String and M Theories, can be found in the *NOVA* mini-series, "The Elegant Universe." [4]

It is sometimes frustrating to be limited by four dimensions. Think about how many books and movies deal with time travel. It is a fascinating topic for science fiction writers and readers. But in our reality, as humans, we can look backwards in time, but we can't go backwards into the past to correct mistakes. Wouldn't it be great to have do-overs? On the other hand, we continuously move forward moment by moment into the future, but can't see with 100 percent accuracy what exactly the future will be! Wouldn't it be great to avoid all mistakes in the future? In truth, because we are four-dimensional limited beings, we can only speculate about the future, as I will describe in detail in the later chapter, THE SPECTRUM OF SPECULATION, (Part III; Chapter 39).

CHAPTER 9

WHY DOES BIBLE PROPHECY WORK?

Unlike human beings, God is not limited by a four-dimensional material world. He is outside of time. This is why Bible prophecy works to accurately foretell future events.

ISAIAH 46:9–10
For I am God, and there is no other; I am God, and there is none like me, *declaring the end from the beginning and from ancient times things not yet done*, saying, 'My counsel shall stand, and I will accomplish all my purpose,' [Bold type and Italics added]

Also consider the following Scripture:

AMOS 3:7
For the Lord GOD does nothing without revealing his secret to his servants the prophets...

Godly wisdom is far superior to the wisdom of man. In addition to being omniscient, all powerful, and infinitely intelligent, God knows our future with

100 percent certainty. This is one of the reasons why we should trust in the wisdom of the LORD. Recall Proverbs 3:5.

PROVERBS 3:5
Trust in the LORD with all your heart, and lean not on your own understanding;

Over 25 percent of the Bible is prophecy. Much of this already has been *literally* fulfilled as documented by history. That which has not yet been fulfilled will occur in the future.

Most people, who study prophecy, are in agreement that they are seeing signs of the Last Days that no previous generations have seen. Some people, who don't study prophecy have not been informed about these signs or have been burned by other people's misinterpretations. And there are other people who dismiss Bible prophecy and consider it fantasy. One of my questions to people who have little knowledge about Bible prophecy is, "How can you assess whether the signs of prophecy are occurring now, if you don't even bother to know what the specific signs are?

It is not within the scope of this book to detail the prophecies that comprise over 25 percent of the Bible. But as mentioned in the introduction of this book, one way of looking at Bible prophecy is as a jigsaw puzzle that contains different categories of puzzle pieces, including geopolitical pieces, technology pieces, religious and social trend pieces, and astronomical pieces. We are still missing some pieces of this puzzle. However, as time moves forward, we will get more pieces and the final look of the puzzle will become more obvious. Part III of this book will throw the numerical puzzle pieces revealed in the book onto the jigsaw assembly table, thereby facilitating an understanding of how the jigsaw pieces from all categories will fit together. I hope that this book will help to clarify how the final completed puzzle will look.

CHAPTER 10

GREEK VERSUS HEBREW?

God authored the entire Bible. It was transcribed by Jewish writers through a Hebraic mindset. The Hebraic mindset is different than the Western Greek mindset, as were their customs and cultures. This difference causes mistranslation, misinterpretation, and confusion seen in today's views of the Bible. It is not the focus of this book to detail these different mindsets, but I do want to point out that if you strive for accuracy in the Bible, it would be beneficial for you to understand the Bible from the original Hebraic mindset. For your benefit, I would refer you to Dr. Richard Booker's two books: *Torah: Law or Grace?* [1] and *How The Cross Became The Sword.*

One aspect of the Greek mindset is that an answer to a question should be foremost based on a logical "yes or no." In the computer digital world, this might be a 0 or a 1, which is fully appropriate for this technology. In contrast, the answer to a question from a Hebraic mindset may yield answer of, "Yes that is correct, but yes that other answer also is correct!" For example, you meet someone who didn't know anything about the geography in North America and you tell him that you are an American. He later hears you telling someone else that you are a Texan. He then asks you why you lied to him. You told him you are an American, but told someone else that you are a Texan. The truth is that both could be true.

Another characteristic of our Greek Western mindset is that we tend to think more linear with respect to time in our lives; always progressing forward. Out with the old, in with the new! An over-reliance on this mindset creates a skewed perception of our reality. It risks an under-appreciation of the cyclical nature of our universe and how this cyclical nature affects us. The Hebraic mindset tends to be more cyclically and seasonally oriented.

ECCLESIASTES 3:1
For everything there is a season, and a time for every matter under heaven:

Humans cannot change their nature by their own efforts. Only God can change one's nature. Human nature by itself does not change from one generation to the next; therefore, we rarely learn from the mistakes other generations have made in the past and we unfortunately continue to repeat them. This will be illustrated in Part III, Chapter 37: THE SEASONS FOR WAR IN THE UNITED STATES OF AMERICA AND WORLD WAR III.

CHAPTER 11

ARE BIBLICAL CHAPTER AND VERSE NUMBERS INSPIRED BY GOD?

The text of the Bible was completed around 96 AD with the book of Revelation. But, chapter and verse numbers were added much later. In the Bible printed today, the chapter numbers were added in the early 1200s AD and the verses were added in the 1500s AD. However, because God is outside of our time dimension, He certainly knew where the chapter and verse numbers would eventually be placed within the Biblical text. So, is there some possible information to be gained from this? I wouldn't focus too much on this topic, but I have come across a few chapter and verse numbers that are a compelling supportive adjunct to the Biblical text. These suggest that the placement of *some* chapter and verse numbers may be God-inspired. I will share some of these with you in various sections of this book.

I once asked a prominent, well-respected Biblical scholar whether he thought chapter and verse numbers were potentially inspired by God. He said absolutely not! He said he knew this because he could prove that contiguous verses found in Isaiah were artificially broken up and therefore the placement of all chapter and verse numbers were solely the additions of man. I thought about his answer and said wait a minute, just because one or two verse numbers seem to be additions of man, this doesn't invalidate the possibility that the placement of *some* of the chapter and verse numbers are God-inspired. This was not a Greek mindset answer of either "Yes, they all are" or "No, they all are not" God-inspired. If God elected to use some of the chapter and verse numbers to communicate to us, who are we to tie His hands with our closed hearts and minds?

Therefore, the placement of some chapter and verse numbers could be inspired by God. He could be using some of them to add additional evidence of validation to the Biblical text. However, this is probably not true of the large majority of these numbers. But, as you read the Biblical text, let God's Holy Spirit be your guide on this subject. Pay attention to all the numbers. Look to see if the placement of the chapter and verse numbers adds meaning or support to the text.

CHAPTER 12

WHICH CALENDAR COULD GOD BE USING TO SPEAK TO US: HEBRAIC OR GREGORIAN?

I have heard several preachers who are helping people rediscover the Jewish roots of their Christian faith, say that, "God doesn't keep time by our Gregorian calendar. He is still using the Jewish calendar, the one that He set up!" Please know that I have the utmost respect for and gratefulness to these preachers who are making great strides in helping us to better understand Christianity, as well as undo much of the Western mindset and error that crept into it, by focusing on the Jewish roots.

But, I want to point out the "here we go again with the Greek Western mindset influence" I talked about in Chapter 10. This is the thought that God could use either Gregorian calendar or Jewish calendar, and not both! Whereas, the Hebraic mindset would consider that maybe both choices are correct.

Please remember that God is outside of time. Way before the Gregorian calendar was in place, as the Biblical text was put into writing, God knew with absolute certainty that the Gregorian calendar was going to be adopted by much of our world. He also knew exactly what the timing of this calendar would be and how this timing would align with the Hebraic calendar.

Therefore, it is possible that God could be using both calendars. But is it probable? In Part II of this book, I will provide compelling evidence that He is using both calendars. And I think it's pretty cool and amazing how these calendars line up with each other and with the numbers in the Bible.

CHAPTER 13

DISPELLING THE COMMON TEACHING THAT NO ONE WILL EVER KNOW WHEN CHRIST WILL RETURN

Over the past twelve years, I have told many people that a major Biblical numerical convergence will occur during the years 2019 to 2020. This will also be the season for World War III, and we may be entering the time frame for Yeshua's return to our earth realm. When I said these things, the most common response I received was that their pastor taught them that no one will ever know when Yeshua will return until it actually happens. They most commonly refer to the words of Yeshua found in the following Biblical passage.

MATTHEW 24:36
But concerning that day and hour no one knows, not even the angels of heaven, nor the Son, but the Father only

Please note: When I first became aware of God's use of numbers, I had no idea that the numerical data I will share with you would end up suggesting a specific season for Yeshua's return. I just started collecting the data. But when I realized that the data suggested a specific season, I decided to look into Matthew 24 more closely.

As human beings, we are most often concerned with *when* something will happen. Much of this focus on *when* something will happen stems from the fact that human beings are four dimensionally limited beings, as I discussed in Chapter 8. If you believe that the stock market will violently crash one day, wouldn't it be nice to know exactly *when* that will happen? If your house is going to be hit by a tornado in the future, wouldn't it be nice to know ahead of time exactly *when* that will happen?

In the Bible, Yeshua's disciples had the same focus on *when*.

MATTHEW 24:3

As he sat on the Mount of Olives, the disciples came to him privately, saying, "Tell us, **when** will these things be, and what will be the sign of your coming and of the end of the age?".
[Bold type and Italics added]

Yeshua proceeded to tell His disciples the signs people would see in the future surrounding the end of the age and His return. However, He told His disciples that they were *not* going to know when! Still undeterred, after Yeshua's crucifixion, resurrection, and just before He ascended into heaven, the disciples asked Him again: *when?!*

ACTS 1:6–7
THE ASCENSION

So when they had come together, they asked him, "Lord, will you *at this time* restore the kingdom to Israel?" [7] He said to them, "It is not for you to know *times or seasons* that the Father has fixed by his own authority. [Italics added]

In Matthew 24, Yeshua alludes to the fact that the people, who see the future signs He was describing, would at least be able to know the *season* of His return. But this was not to be true for His disciples. As described above in Acts 1, *these* disciples would *not* even get to know the times or seasons!

So, even though we, as humans, really want to know when Yeshua will return, God really *deemphasizes* when this will happen. It is not too difficult to understand why He may do this. For us, if we knew Yeshua wasn't going to return until many years in the future, we might very well stray away from His commandments to even greater extremes than we have done as individuals and as a society. However, the moment we die as individuals, that moment is the end of days' event for us. There are no do-overs after we die.

HEBREWS 9:27

It is appointed for man to die once, and after that comes judgment

Now those people who say no one will ever know when Yeshua will return until it happens have a very strong argument on their side. They have always been 100 percent correct in the past! The list of people and groups who have wrongly predicted when Christ will return is huge, and I am well familiar with this. However, just because in the past people who have asserted that no one will be able to know the day or hour of Yeshua's return have always been correct, does this mean they will always be correct in the future? Is it still possible that God might allow some in the very last generation to know approximately when He will return? Let's examine this possibility in some detail.

First, we need to look at *the precise verb tense* for the word "knows" in Matthew 24:36. God is very careful and precise in His Word. He will never contradict Himself. I reexamined this verse in the original language it was written: Greek. For convenience, here it is again in English.

MATTHEW 24:36
But concerning that day and hour no one *knows*, not even the angels of heaven, nor the Son, but the Father only [Italics added]

In Greek, the word corresponding to the English word "knows" is solely in the *present tense*. And note that the verse does *not* say, "no one knows and no one will *ever* know the day or the hour." Speaking in the present tense, Yeshua was specifically referring only to the time frame that He was talking with His disciples directly in front of Him.

Second, the book of Daniel foretells that a group of people who are alive on this Earth just prior to the return of Yeshua, will know the day when He will return. Like Yeshua's disciples and most other believers, even Daniel, a great prophet, wanted to know *when* the end of days would be. He also was told *NO*. He needed to go his way. He would not be told when the end of days was going to be. However, he was also told that the understanding of when the end events were to occur *would be* known or unsealed at the time of the end. The last "time, times, and a half of time" seen in the verse below equals the last 3.5 years.

DANIEL 12:6–9

"How long shall it be till the end of these wonders?" And I heard the man clothed in linen, who was above the waters of the stream; he raised his right hand and his left hand toward heaven and swore by him who lives forever that it would be for *a time, times, and half a time*, and that when the shattering of the power of the holy people comes to an end *all these things would be finished*. I heard, but I did not understand. Then I said, "O my lord, what shall be the outcome of these things?" He said, "Go your way, Daniel, for *the words are shut up and sealed until the time of the end.* [Italics added]

The "time of the end" refers to the end of the age of human government and not the end of the world.

The Bible clearly states that the world will never end. However, "time of the end" will be the end of the world as we have known it. The understanding of when Yeshua will return will no longer remain sealed up approximately 3.5 years before He actually returns.

To further substantiate the preceding assertion, note that in the very same chapter of Matthew 24, in which Yeshua stated in the present tense "no one knows," Yeshua *validated* the words spoken by the prophet Daniel.

MATTHEW 24:15–16
The Abomination of Desolation "So when you see *the abomination of desolation spoken of by the prophet Daniel,* standing in the holy place (let the reader understand), then let those who are in Judea flee to the mountains" [Italics added]

So let's now look at Daniel 12 further, where the abomination of desolation is also described. In the following verse, a specific number of days is given between the abomination of desolation and the time of the end of human government, when Messiah will return to rule the Earth.

DANIEL 12:11
And from the time that the regular burnt offering is taken away and *the abomination that makes desolate* is set up, there shall be 1,290 days. [Italics added]

So both Yeshua and Daniel talk about an event referred to as the abomination of desolation. Yeshua validates the words of Daniel. And Daniel states there shall be a countdown of a specific number of days! Therefore, Yeshua validates that there will be a specific numbers of days counting down from the abomination of desolation to His return and that the knowledge of this event *would be* known or unsealed at the time of the end. For reference, 1,290 days is 30 days longer than 3.5 years in the Jewish calendar of 360 days per year.

My third and final point focuses on *a Jewish idiom* concerning the meaning of "the day and hour that no one knows" and on *the Jewish fall feast period.* If I were to say to you in this day and age that someone "kicked the bucket," you would probably know that I was saying that someone died, and not that someone literally kicked a bucket for some reason. This is a modern-day idiom. On the other hand, if you were able to go back in time 2,000 years and you told people that someone kicked the bucket, they wouldn't know what you were talking about. It is my understanding from the study of Hebraic roots of the Christian faith that if you were back in the time of Yeshua and of His disciples, and you said to someone, "I'll see you in Jerusalem during the festival *when no one knows the day or hour*!" They probably would have responded, "OK. I'll see you in Jerusalem during the fall feast holidays!" The saying, "no one knows the day or hour" was a common Jewish idiom that referred to the time of the Fall Feast holiday period.

Rosh Hashanah is the beginning of the Jewish civil calendar year and of the fall feast holiday period. The Jewish *civil* calendar is a different calendar than the Jewish *religious* calendar, which starts in the spring on the first day of the Jewish month Nisan. During the time of Yeshua and of His disciples, no human knew, ahead of time, the *exact timing* of the beginning of Rosh Hashanah, because it was determined by the Jewish high court after hearing the testimony of witnesses. These witnesses would testify that they saw the first thin crescent of the moon in Jerusalem. That exact hour would vary each year. The exact day would also vary from year to year, but would be within a two-day period. Today Rosh Hashanah is observed as a two-day holiday as an enactment of the early prophets. [5]

Every year, this fall feast period spans twenty-one to twenty-two days, and it actually contains three separate feasts. The last of the three fall feasts is also the last of seven feasts of the Jewish *religious* calendar year. This seventh and last feast is called *The Feast of Tabernacles*, which is also known as *Sukkot*. This feast spans seven to eight days. Sukkot is when *God dwells with us*. Also, its position as the last and seventh Jewish feast of the Jewish religious calendar symbolizes a completed act of God in our earth realm. Likewise, when Yeshua returns, man's government will end. The number 7 will be explained in Part II, Chapter 15.

Many prominent Biblical scholars of today make strong arguments that significant parallels exist between the Jewish fall feast period and the future return of Yeshua, the Messiah. In these arguments, the Jewish fall feast period is not only a memorial of the past, but is also a rehearsal for the future. In addition to the strong arguments made by Biblical scholars, *numerically* speaking, because Sukkot is associated with the number 7, the time period *between* the sixth feast, Yom Kippur, and the end of the seventh feast, Sukkot, of some future year, will be the most likely time window when Messiah will return. A *6 to 7* transition represents a transition from man to God (see Part II, Chapter 31).

The time between the sixth feast and the last day of the seventh feast is *twelve* days. This time of transition would seem to make the most sense, because it is consistent with how God uses these numbers: Not only does *6 to 7* represent a transition from man to God, but also 12 represents a divine government (see Part II, Chapter 23). When Yeshua returns, He will set up His divine government on this Earth. The hypothetical speculative model presented later in this book will include a hypothetical Jewish fall feast return as a significant time window to which we should pay special attention.

In conclusion, it has been 100 percent true in the past that no one has foretold precisely when Yeshua will return. However, do not allow this truth of past history to completely close your mind about the future. It is at least possible and maybe even probable that multitudes of people in the future may be able to know when He will return; perhaps at least within a time window of twelve days and maybe down to the day, based upon the 1,290-day countdown written in Daniel and Yeshua's validation thereof. I have no evidence to suggest that anyone will ever know the exact hour, however.

I cannot see the future; however, I can envision a possible scenario in which World War III will happen, followed by the event known as the abomination of desolation. From that point forward a countdown of 1,290 days would begin. At that specific time, all the disagreement among scholars would be a moot point. Then the great tribulation would be upon this Earth and we will all have much greater concerns.

PART II

HOW GOD USES NUMBERS IN THE BIBLE AND IN THE WORLD AROUND US TODAY

I n Part II of this book, the information on numbers and numerical patterns are not presented in numerical order. Rather, the information is presented in the approximate order it was obtained and/or in an order that this author believes is best suited to help the reader understand the numbers presented in subsequent chapters. This order will build a base of knowledge that will be essential to fully understanding the speculative hypothetical model presented in Part III of this book.

Some of the following chapters are *extremely* brief, whereas others are much more extensive because they often include anecdotal stories about how the numbers or numerical patterns were obtained. One of the main purposes of this book is to present original insight into how God may be using numbers to speak to us. This book is not meant to be an exhaustive detailed examination of all Biblical numbers.

CHAPTER 14

THE NUMBER ONE (1)

The most important aspect of the number "1" in the Bible is that there is only *one* God.

DEUTERONOMY 6:4
Hear, O Israel: The LORD our God, the LORD
is **one**! [Bold type added]

Also equally important is the commandment that we put God number 1; *first* in everything we do.

DEUTERONOMY 5:7
(The first of the Ten Commandments)
You shall have no other gods before Me.

CHAPTER 15

THE NUMBER SEVEN (7)

The number 7 is the most commonly recognized number in the Bible. The Bible is replete with its use. It represents *a completed act of perfection by God in the earth realm*. As described in Part I of this book, the earth realm is our material world; the four dimensional reality that we can physically perceive. It is important to distinguish and contrast the number 7 from the number 3. Both numbers represent *completion*. However, when God completes an act in the *spirit* realm, it is most often associated with the number 3. The number 3 will be discussed in detail in Part II, Chapter 17.

Here are just a few examples of the number 7 that can be easily found in the Bible:

- God created the earth in *7 days*. (Genesis 1 and 2)

- God defined that there be *7* days *in a week* as can be seen in the 4th of the Ten Commandments. (Exodus 20:11)

Isn't it interesting that today a standard of time measurement is a week defined to be 7 days? God could have chosen a different number. Why not 10, for example? After all, we have 10 fingers and 10 toes. We could have defined a week to contain 10 days. The fact that we have 7 days in a week is not a random occurrence. There is a purpose and consistency by the Great Designer that I hope you will appreciate as you continue to read this book.

There are 7 trumpets, 7 seals, and 7 bowls in the book of Revelation. All of these describe judgments that will be completed acts of God in our *earth* realm.

Here are just two examples of the number 7 that can be easily seen in our earth realm today:

- The earth God created today contains *7 continents*.

- Coincidence? I don't believe that the ancient Israelites knew that there were 7 continents on the earth.

- Today there are approximately *7 billion people* who live on this Earth.

It is projected that by 2016 that the Earth will have approximately *7.4* billion people.[6]

It is also interesting that the US government is currently spending *$7.04* million per second. I have no evidence to suggest that God is marking some sort of completion in the earth realm with this; this may just be an example of someone, in this case me, attributing a specific significance to a number in which specific significance does not play out. But, I thought it important to mention this now, in late 2015 – before the year 2016, in case our government goes into some form of default in 2016.

CHAPTER 16

THE NUMBER SIX (6)

The number 6 is the number *given to man by God* and/or *to the imperfect efforts of man*. In our material earth realm, man's efforts, represented by 6, fall short of God's perfection, represented by the number 7. Falling short of God's perfection in the earth realm can also be represented by 6 multiplied by a factor of 10, such as in *60* or *600*, etc.

Here are some examples of the number 6 as used in the Bible.

- **Man was created on the 6th day.**

GENESIS 1:26–27, 31
Then God said, "Let Us make man in Our image, according to Our likeness; . . . So God created man in His *own* image; in the image of God He created him; male and female He created them. . . . Then God saw everything that He had made, and indeed *it was* very good. So the evening and the morning were the **sixth day**.
[Bold type and Italics added]

- **Man was to labor for 6 days.**

EXODUS 20:9
Six days you shall labor and do all your work,
[Bold type and Italics added]

DEUTERONOMY 5:13
Six days you shall labor and do all your work,
[Bold type and Italics added]

- **Pharaoh's efforts to chase after and kill the Israelites who left Egypt fell woefully short of success. This effort of man was also marked with a label of a 6; in this case, 600.**

EXODUS 14:5–7
Now it was told the king of Egypt that the people had fled, and the heart of Pharaoh and his servants was turned against the people; and they said, "Why have we done this, that we have let Israel go from serving us?" So he made ready his chariot and took his people with him. Also, he took *six hundred* choice chariots, and all the chariots of Egypt with captains over every one of them. [Bold type and Italics added]

Now, if you had read this passage from the Bible for the very first time and you knew ahead of time that God uses a number 6 to represent an effort of man that fails or falls short of God's perfection in the earth realm and then you saw the number 600, you might highly suspect that Pharaoh's effort to stop the Israelites was doomed to fail.

I wouldn't be surprised if God actually orchestrated the number of chariots to equal *600*. Perhaps Pharaoh originally had 650 chariots, but 50 of them, unexpected to the Egyptians, had mechanical problems. If any variation of this is true, then perhaps God orchestrated this not to reassure the fleeing Israelites that they would be OK in light of the fact that 600 chariots were attacking them, but rather *for you* today, so that you can see God's consistency in how He uses numbers.

- **The 600,000 Israelite men left Egypt in the Exodus. They fell short of God's plan.**

As a group, they fell short of the plan God originally had for them. God chose the timing of the Exodus. At this time, the Israelites left Egypt with *600,000* men. This resulted, among other punishments, in a 40-year extended wandering in the desert before God allowed them to enter the Promised Land.

EXODUS 12:37

Then the children of Israel journeyed from Rameses to Succoth, about **_six hundred thousand_** men on foot, besides children. [Bold type and Italics added]

God knew ahead of time that the efforts of this group would fall short in terms of their obedience to Him.

- **The most infamous number given to a man contains three 6s: 666.**

REVELATION 13:16–18

He causes all, both small and great, rich and poor, free and slave, to receive a **mark** on their right hand or on their foreheads, and that no one may **buy or sell** except one who has the mark or the name of the beast, or the number of his name. Here is wisdom. Let him who has understanding calculate the number of the beast, for it is the number of a man: His number *is* **666**. [Bold type added]

It appears probable that God has assigned the number 666 to be associated with the Antichrist, a man who will come on the world scene and *force* everyone to buy and sell with a number. Never before in human history has this even been technologically possible. Only the generations still alive today have experienced worldwide buying and selling with numbers, e.g. credit cards. This system is now being put into place. The Antichrist will most likely use future dire events as an excuse to outlaw all forms of cash currency. The result will be a "cashless" society. If you do not abide by the bidding of the controlling worldly authorities, you will not be able to buy gas for your car, buy food, or pay your bills. You will not even be able to keep your house, regardless if it is completely paid for or not, because you will not be able to pay the taxes on it without accepting the mark. The government might then just steal your house.

But take heart, the Bible teaches that this system will not be implemented until after the event of the abomination of desolation. The maximum time that this system will be in place is 3.5 years.

However, the Bible is also very clear that if you choose to accept this mark, this is equivalent to saying that your money is the god of your life and is of higher importance than the One True God. This is a huge problem for the unwise: God will not have any gods above Him. According to the Bible, if you choose to accept this mark, eternal damnation will be your fate. This is His first commandment:

EXODUS 20:3
You shall have no other gods before Me.

Here is the verse that tells of the fate of those who take the mark. This is a warning of judgment against a group of unwise people. A future *chapter* and *verse number* 9/11 of sorts; (see also the Chapters on 9 and 11)

REVELATION 14:9–11
If anyone worships the beast and its image and receives *a mark on his forehead or on his hand*, he also will drink the wine of God's wrath, poured full strength into the cup of his anger, and

he will be tormented with fire and sulfur in the presence of the holy angels and in the presence of the Lamb. ***And the smoke of their torment goes up forever and ever, and they have no rest, day or night, these worshipers of the beast and its image, and whoever receives the mark of its name.*** [Bold type and Italics added]

The "beast" is another name for the Antichrist. We do not yet know for sure who this man will be, but at the time of God's choosing, God says in Revelation 13 those with understanding will be able to calculate this number.

There is another use of 666 also associated with a form of *money*. You may find this interesting. It is found in the First Testament.

1 KINGS 10:14
SOLOMON'S GREAT WEALTH

The weight of **gold** that came to Solomon yearly was **six hundred and sixty-six** talents of gold, [Bold type added]

In addition to the interpretation of being able to buy and sell with numbers, some scholars recently have discovered that the original Greek text corresponding to the English translation of 666 may also have a *symbolic translation in the Arabic language*. This interpretation may also turn out to be valid. Both may be valid. Walid Shoebat, a former Muslim and now a Christian and Bible scholar, has identified this. To understand this, please do a web search on "Walid Shoebat explains 666".[7]

Here is something else that you may find interesting along the line of the number 666, in association with digital technology and a cashless society. The first Apple computer, the Apple I, went on sale during the month of the American bicentennial in July of 1976 for the price of $666.66. I have found no evidence that Steve Wozniak specifically wanted to make any kind of statement on the mark of the beast; According to my reading, he liked repeating digits and $666.66 was a one-third markup price from the $500 wholesale price.[8]

We do not have all the pieces of this puzzle to identify this mark precisely. At this time, exact identification, by the general public, won't be possible until after the abomination of desolation occurs.

Here are some other examples of the number 6 or derivatives thereof that can be seen in our earth realm today.

- **The most common unit by which a man's labor is compensated is by the hour, which is *60 minutes*.**

Isn't it interesting that God commanded the Israelites to work for *6*-day time periods and that we most commonly compensate man's labor by a period of *60 minutes*? Being a numbers person, I think so. It is also interesting and consistent with God's use of the number 6 that we then divide every minute up into *60 seconds*.

- ## It has been approximately 6,000 years since the time of Adam and Eve.

Many who study Bible prophecy have noted that it has been approximately *6,000 years* since the time of Adam and Eve. They suggest that 6,000 years may be a numerical timing marker for the return of Yeshua. This suggestion is derived from a combination of two facts. First, the number God has assigned to man is 6 and man falls short of His perfection in the earth realm. Second, is the fact that *a day is like a thousand years* to the Lord (2 Peter 3:8). From these two facts, comes the interpretation that man's governmental dominion on the earth most probably will end near the completion of the 6,000-year period since Adam and Eve: 6 x 1,000 = 6,000. If true, mankind will have been given 6,000 years of time, during which it could choose to live and govern with or apart from God and His commandments. According to the Bible, despite its best efforts, mankind will eventually fail, thus proving that it and the entire earth cannot survive apart from God. Humans and their inherent sin will bring the world to the very brink of total destruction. A failure of mankind, in this regard, at a time close to the 6000-year period since Adam and Eve is consistent with how God uses numbers and is consistent with the majority of major signs that can be seen easily in the world today. This topic will be discussed more fully in the Part II, Chapter 31; *The Transition Pattern of 6 to 7*. In addition, I am writing this text in October 2015, which in the Hebraic calendar is in the year 5,776, which is close to 6,000 years, yet still *224* years away. This difference from 6,000 years will also be discussed in Part III.

- **Modern examples of the number 6 in which we can see world governments failing.**

Have you ever noticed, as I have, that when the world powers hold meetings to stop the proliferation of WMD's (Weapons of Mass Destruction), they always seem to be labeled in terms of *six-party talks*? Consistent with the number 6, these talks have proven to be efforts of men that have utterly failed. I remember back in 2003, when six-party talks began with North Korea, I thought "*Six-party*? That looks like it's destined to fail!" These six-party talks were a series of multilateral negotiations held intermittently since 2003 and attended by China, Japan, North Korea, Russia, South Korea, and the United States for the purpose of dismantling North Korea's nuclear program. North Korea was counted as one of the *six* parties.

Consistent with the number *6* and a failed effort of man, the *six-party* talks failed miserably! Not only did North Korea refuse to dismantle their nuclear program, they conducted their first successful nuclear explosion in 2009.

So what did the world powers next decide to do with Iran? Talks with Iran had to be labeled with a form of a number 6, of course! Really? So get this: On *June 6, 2006* or 06/06/06, China, France, Germany, Russia, the United Kingdom, and the United States proposed a framework agreement to Iran offering incentives for Iran to halt its enrichment program for an indefinite period of time. The group of nations making this proposal was labeled "*P5+1*", referring to the five permanent members of the UN Security Council and Germany. To me, "P5+1" was just another labeling of a group of six nations. And over the years since 2006, I have most commonly seen and heard the Iranian nuclear talks referred to by the news media as six-party talks. What is the world government's love affair with *6s*?

The very observant reader will note a difference in the number of countries involved in the six-party North Korean talks vs. the six-party Iranian talks. The latter set of talks does not include Iran in the count yielding six parties. If you include Iran, there are actually *seven* countries. But here is the bigger point: The world still *elected* to refer the Iranian talks as *six-party* talks! Did God orchestrate the labeling of these doomed talks with a 6 to speak to us? The talks certainly have failed and most likely will contribute to our path to World War III.

Here are two examples of the news media labeling the Iranian nuclear talks as six-party talks.

"Russia and Iran to work on resumption of **six-party talks**"
Published: November 12, 2006, 00:00
Moscow: Russia and Iran will try to resume **six-party** talks on Iran's nuclear programme, Russia's Foreign Minister Sergei Lavrov said on Saturday after President Vladimir Putin met Iran's nuclear envoy.

The **six powers** - the United States, Britain, China, France, Russia and Germany - made a proposal in June for economic, technological and political cooperation if Iran halted work the West suspects is designed to produce atomic weapons, but Tehran insists is for electricity generation. [9] [Bold type added]

A TRIP TO THE UNITED NATIONS AND THE NUMBER 6.

One of the first anecdotal experiences I had receiving numerical revelation about the number 6 involved a trip to the UN. Before we left the USA on a 2004 tour to Israel, we stopped at the United Nations in New York City. It seems clear to many who study Bible prophecy that this organization is the most likely candidate to be the *one world government* that the Bible symbolically foretells of. It embodies the collective efforts of man to govern the earth, mostly under the pretense of saving the Earth. According to the Bible, world government falls woefully short of success and takes the world to the very brink of total destruction. Hence, as an effort of man that falls short of God's perfection, world government as represented by the UN should have a 6 associated with it.

At the UN building, our tour guide sat a group of us down in the room where the UN General Assembly meets. The first thing she said to us was, "Does anyone here know how many languages that we speak in this world?" We all looked at each other perplexed and wondered why she asked. But nobody knew the answer.

She then said, "We speak about *6,000* languages on this Earth." She then pointed to the enclosed glass booths about the upper perimeter of the room and said, "Anyone can speak any one of those *6,000* languages before the Security Council and our translators will simultaneously translate into *6* languages."

The numbers began slamming into my consciousness, especially since I knew that the world population that spoke those *6,000* languages was approximately *6 billion* at that time. I wondered to myself, "Why they didn't choose 5, 7, or 10 languages? Why did it have to be *another* 6?" Still, I remained quiet. The tour guide then proceeded to tell us that the whole of the UN was much greater than the UN General Assembly we saw represented before us. She proudly said, "With the addition of the UN World Court in July 2002, the entire UN is actually made up of *6* separate entities!" At that point, I looked around at our group and saw that nobody else was picking up on the numbers. So I raised my hand to ask a question for the purpose of making the numbers clear to all in our group. I said, "You mean to tell me that this world containing *6 billion* people speak *6,000* languages and you the UN, now made up of *6* separate entities, have electively chosen to translate into *6 languages*?" When I verbalized the *series of 6s* associated with the United Nations, all in our tour group got it. The only one who did not understand was the proud tour guide.

The United Nation's love for the number 6 is perhaps God's way of numerically labeling it. It is a numerical confirmation that the UN is an effort of man that will fall short of God's perfection and intention. It also goes a long way to indicate that the UN will be the basis for the one world government formation foretold of in the Bible.

My trip to the UN was back in 2004. Today in 2015, the UN is still made up of 6 main entities.

CHAPTER 17

THE NUMBER THREE (3)

od uses the number 7 to represent His completed act in the *earth* realm. But what if the "act of God" occurs in the *spirit* realm? The answer to this question highlights the *difference* between how God uses the number 7 and the number 3.

God uses of *both* number 3 and number 7 as numbers of *completion*. However, when God completes an act in the *spirit* realm, it is most often associated with the number 3; whereas, when God completes an act of perfection in the *earth* realm, it is most often associated with the number 7.

Completed acts of God in the *spirit* realm are also associated with God's Holy Spirit. The Holy Spirit is the *3rd* manifestation of the *one true* God. Completed acts of God that are associated with the Holy Spirit are clearly seen throughout the book of Acts. This book describes the Holy Spirit and is full of number 3 usages! Examples from the book of Acts are included later in this chapter.

But before we look at examples of God's use of the number 3 in the Bible, let's look at the simple mathematical equation $3 + 4 = 7$. God first declares something in the spirit realm (3). It then spreads to the 4 corners of the earth for a perfect completion of His will in the earth realm (7). Hence, $3 + 4 = 7$ is a numerical representative of the *order of completion* from the spirit to the earth realm. The number 4 will be discussed more fully in the next chapter.

Did you ever wonder why Peter denied Christ 3 times, and why Christ was resurrected after 3 days and 3 nights? This chapter will explain these.

Here are some examples of the number 3 as used in the Bible to represent a spiritual completion.

Some examples of the number 3 from the First Testament:

- **God commanded Israelite males to attend 3 spiritual feasts per year.**

EXODUS 23:14, 17
Three times you shall keep a feast to Me in the year: *Three times* in the year all your males *shall appear before the Lord GOD*. [Bold type and Italics added]

Appearing three times per year before the Lord symbolized a completion in the *spiritual* realm; *not* a completion in the physical earthly realm. Showing up physically for the feasts didn't matter if the people's spiritual hearts weren't in favor of being there. This lesson can also be applied today, when people just physically show up to church and do not have their hearts into being there.

- **Esther and the Jews fasted for 3 days and 3 nights. This was a spiritual act that changed the fate for the Jews from being totally annihilated to being victorious.**

ESTHER 4:15–16
ESTHER AGREES TO HELP THE JEWS

Then Esther told them to reply to Mordecai, "Go, gather all the Jews to be found in Susa, and hold a fast on my behalf, and do not eat or drink for **three days**, night or day. I and my young women will also fast as you do. Then I will go to the king, though it is against the law, and if I perish, I perish." [Bold type added]

The memory of this huge reversal of historical events that was initiated by a 3, a completion in the spirit realm, is still celebrated every year in modern times today. This celebration is known as *Purim*.

- **God chose to come down from the spirit realm upon Mount Sinai on the 3rd day of the 3rd month after they left Egypt.**

EXODUS 19:1, 10–11 (NKJV)
ISRAEL AT MOUNT SINAI

in the **third** month after the children of Israel had gone out of the land of Egypt, on the same day*, they came to the Wilderness of Sinai.

[added *: this was the first day of the month]
Then the LORD said to Moses, "Go to
the people and consecrate them today and
tomorrow, and let them wash their clothes.
And let them be ready for the **third** day.
For on the **third** day the LORD will come down
upon Mount Sinai in the sight of all the people.
[Bold type added]

Note that God chose to come down from the spirit
realm upon Mount Sinai on the *3rd* day of the *3rd*
month after they left Egypt. Even though this timing
of day and month occurs in the earth realm, God
numerically tells the Israelites and us that He was going
to do something that involved *spiritual completion*. The
number 3 represents this.

- **Here is an example, in which God
  uses *both* the numbers 3 and 7 to
  represent completion.**

In the Book of Numbers, Chapter 19, God uses the
number 3 to represent a completion of purification first
in the *spirit* realm and then the number 7 to represent
completion of purification in the *earth* realm.

NUMBERS 19:11–13

Whoever touches the dead body of any person
shall be unclean **seven** days. He shall cleanse
himself with the water on the **third** day and on
the **seventh** day, and so be clean. But if he does
not cleanse himself on the **third** day and on the

seventh day, he will not become clean. Whoever touches a dead person, the body of anyone who has died, and does not cleanse himself, defiles the tabernacle of the LORD, [Bold type added]

It's important to be purified first in your heart, your spiritual realm (3), before you can be of good service to Him in the earth realm (7).

- **Gideon's Valiant Three Hundred (3 x 100)**

This example is a particularly interesting section of Scripture because God gives Gideon victory over an enemy army through the *spirit realm* (3). The enemy was spiritually led to fight and kill each other. As such, the story appropriately contains many 3s. God or the Israelites did not *physically* kill the enemy. In this example, God completes His act by using the number 3 as a base and then magnifies the effect *a hundredfold*.

JUDGES 7:2–8, 12, 15–22
GIDEON'S VALIANT THREE HUNDRED

And the LORD said to Gideon, "The people who are with you are too many for Me to give the Midianites into their hands, lest Israel claim glory for itself against Me, saying, 'My own hand has saved me.' Now therefore, proclaim in the hearing of the people, saying, 'Whoever is fearful and afraid, let him turn and depart at once from Mount Gilead.'" And twenty-two thousand of the people returned, and ten thousand remained.

But the LORD said to Gideon, "The people are still too many; bring them down to the water, and I will test them for you there. Then it will be, that of whom I say to you, 'This one shall go with you,' the same shall go with you; and of whomever I say to you, 'This one shall not go with you,' the same shall not go." So he brought the people down to the water. And the LORD said to Gideon, "Everyone who laps from the water with his tongue, as a dog laps, you shall set apart by himself; likewise everyone who gets down on his knees to drink." And the number of those who lapped, putting their hand to their mouth, was **three hundred** men; but all the rest of the people got down on their knees to drink water.

Then the LORD said to Gideon, "By the **three hundred** men who lapped I will save you, and deliver the Midianites into your hand. Let all the other people go, every man to his place." So the people took provisions and their trumpets in their hands. And he sent away all the rest of Israel, every man to his tent, and retained those **three hundred** men.

Now the camp of Midian was below him in the valley. . . . Now the Midianites and Amalekites, all the people of the East, were lying in the valley as numerous as locusts; and their camels were without number, as the sand by the seashore in multitude. . . .

And so it was, when Gideon heard the telling of the dream and its interpretation, that he worshiped. He returned to the camp of Israel, and said, "Arise, for the LORD has delivered the camp of Midian into your hand." Then he divided the **three hundred** men into **three** companies, and he put a trumpet into every man's hand, with empty pitchers, and torches inside the pitchers. And he said to them, "Look at me and do likewise; watch, and when I come to the edge of the camp you shall do as I do: when I blow the trumpet, I and all who are with me, then you also blow the trumpets on every side of the whole camp, and say, 'The sword of the LORD and of Gideon!'"

So Gideon and the hundred men who were with him came to the outpost of the camp at the beginning of the middle watch, just as they had posted the watch; and they blew the trumpets and broke the pitchers that were in their hands. Then the **three** companies blew the trumpets and broke the pitchers—they held the torches in their left hands and the trumpets in their right hands for blowing—and they cried, "The sword of the LORD and of Gideon!"

And every man stood in his place all around the camp; and the whole army ran and cried out and fled. When the **three hundred** blew the trumpets, *the LORD set everyman's sword against his companion throughout the whole camp*; and the army fled to Beth Acacia, toward Zererah, as far as the border of Abel Meholah, by Tabbath. [Bold type and Italics added]

If God *physically* killed the enemy of the Israelites, this would have been a completed act of God in the earth realm and probably represented by a 7. Perhaps God would have thrown lightning bolts 7 times or had the 7 plagues kill the army and made them scatter. But instead, God completed an act in the *spirit realm* (3) by affecting the hearts of the enemy soldiers to become so angry with each other. Therefore, the act was accomplished by a factor of 3. Pretty cool way God uses numbers, huh?

Some examples of the number 3 from the Second Testament:

- **The spiritual ministry of Yeshua (Jesus) was complete after 3 years.**

- **Yeshua (Jesus) was resurrected after 3 days and 3 nights.**

The resurrection of Yeshua was an act of God completed in the *spirit* realm, not in the *earth* realm. As such, it is associated with God's use of the number 3.

LUKE 24: 5–7
HE IS RISEN

"Why do you seek the living among the dead? He is not here, but is risen! Remember how He spoke to you when He was still in Galilee, saying, 'The Son of Man must be delivered into the hands of sinful men, and be crucified, and the **third day** rise again.'" [Bold type added]

- **Yeshua (Jesus) said that Peter would deny Him *three* times. This was a spiritual denial in his heart.**

MATTHEW 26:34–35

Jesus said to him, "Assuredly, I say to you that this night, before the rooster crows, you will deny Me **three** times." Peter said to Him, "Even if I have to die with You, I will not deny You!" [Bold type added]

But despite Peter's claim that he would not deny Yeshua (Jesus) even once, Peter did deny Him *three* times that very night.

MATTHEW 26:75

Immediately a rooster crowed. Then Peter remembered the word Jesus had spoken: "Before the rooster crows, you will disown me **three** times." And he went outside and wept bitterly. [Bold type added]

- **The apostle Paul was blinded for *three* days before he was spiritually converted by receiving the Holy Spirit.**

The apostle Paul's birth name was Saul. He was a Jewish Pharisee on a zealous mission to persecute all Christians. He thought he was doing the right godly thing. But something very dramatic changed his heart and entire life, as seen below.

ACTS 9:3–8 (NKJV)
THE DAMASCUS ROAD: SAUL SPIRITUALLY CONVERTED

As he journeyed he came near Damascus, and suddenly a light shone around him from heaven. Then he fell to the ground, and heard a voice saying to him, "Saul, Saul, why are you persecuting Me?" And he said, "Who are You, Lord?" Then the Lord said, **"I am Jesus**, whom you are persecuting. It *is* hard for you to kick against the goads." [added note: Goad = An agent or means of prodding or urging; a stimulus.] So he, trembling and astonished, said, "Lord, what do You want me to do?" Then the Lord *said* to him, "Arise and go into the city, and you will be told what you must do." And the men who journeyed with him stood speechless, hearing a voice but seeing no one. Then Saul arose from the ground, and when his eyes were opened he saw no one. But they led him by the hand and brought *him* into Damascus. And he was **three days**

without sight, and neither ate nor drank.
[Bold type added]

Saul was physically blinded for *3 days*. He received his physical sight back only after he was spiritually converted by receiving the Holy Spirit.

ACTS 9:17–18 (NKJV)

And Ananias went his way and entered the house; and laying his hands on him he said, "Brother Saul, the Lord Jesus, who appeared to you on the road as you came, has sent me that you may receive your sight and be filled with **the Holy Spirit**." Immediately there fell from his eyes *something* like scales, **and he received his sight at once**; and he arose and was baptized. [Bold type added]

Not only did Saul (now Paul) receive his *physical* sight back, but also his *spiritual eyes* were now opened. And he was able to see spiritually the truth of God and the spirit realm. As alluded to earlier in this book, spiritual blindness is the type of blindness that the lyrics of "**Amazing Grace**" refer to.

Amazing Grace, how sweet the sound,
That saved a wretch like me.
I once was lost but now am found,
Was blind, but now, I see.

- **The Holy Spirit educated Paul for 3 years before God allowed him to begin his ministry.**

Despite the fact that Paul's heart was spiritually converted after *3 days*, he did not immediately begin his ministry. Before Paul began preaching, God's Holy Spirit had to spiritually educate him. This took *3 years*.

GALATIANS 1: 11–12, 15–18 (NKJV)

But I make known to you, brethren, that the gospel which was preached by me is not according to man. For I neither received it from man, nor was I taught *it*, **but *it came* through the revelation of Jesus Christ. . . .**But *when* **it pleased God**, who . . . called *me* through His grace, to reveal His Son in me, that I might preach Him among the Gentiles, I did not immediately confer with flesh and blood, nor did I go up to Jerusalem to those *who were* apostles before me; but I went to Arabia, and returned again to Damascus. Then *after* **three years** I went up to Jerusalem to see Peter [Bold type and Italics added]

- **The Apostle Peter's *spiritual* vision from God was *complete* after *God* repeated a symbolic event *3 separate* times.**

ACTS 10: 10–11, 16 (NKJV)
PETER'S VISION

he [Peter] fell into a trance and saw heaven opened and an object like a great sheet bound at the **four** corners, descending to him and let down to the **earth**. . . . This was done ***three*** times. And the object was taken **up into heaven** again. [Bold type and Italics added]

In Peter's vision he saw a 4-cornered sheet descend down *from heaven* (spirit realm) to the earth and back *three* separate times before the vision was completed. This was a *spiritual* vision from God that was *completed* after *three* times. This vision foreshadowed that Holy Spirit would be made available to all people in the earth who desired Him. This invitation is to be spread to the 4 corners of the earth. (See also the next chapter on the number 4).

Here are two examples of the number 3 that might be operative in our earth realm today. Remember that this book looks at how God is using numbers in the Bible and how they may be operative in the world today.

- It is interesting to note that many of those in the Church who spend much time in prayer say that the most effective time of prayer occurs at *3:00 AM*.

- Although I am not suggesting in any way that the following are completed acts of God in the spirit realm, it is still also interesting to note that many of our common sayings seem *natural* to declare *three* times. Because we are *spiritual beings*, perhaps we sense in our spirits that these declarations are *complete* only after they are said *three* times. I have selected examples that may be recognized by different generational age groups.

For example, "Judy, Judy, Judy" is associated with impersonations of the famous actor Cary Grant. Though Grant may not have ever said this line in a movie, the saying still remains stuck in the consciousness of many. If it had been said only once or twice, this saying probably would not have lasted in our consciousness for so many generations. In an episode of the 1970s TV show *The Brady Bunch*, the name "Marcia" was repeated *three* times. "Marcia, Marcia, Marcia!" This saying probably would not still be in the minds of many forty years later if "Marcia" had been said only twice or even four times.

Likewise, in the 1988 movie *Beetlejuice*, the name "Beetlejuice" had to be said *three* times for a magic saying to work. "Beetlejuice! Beetlejuice! Beetlejuice!" It just would not have sounded complete if it was said only two times. And finally, for the younger generations of readers of this book, in the TV show, *The Big Bang Theory*, Sheldon knocks *three* times on Penny's door, *three* different times while saying "Penny, Penny, Penny!" There are plenty of *YouTube* videos available showing the Penny knock.

CHAPTER 18

THE NUMBER FOUR (4)

God commonly uses the number 4 to symbolize *the earth realm*. He also seems to use it to describe something that *starts* in one place on the *earth* and then eventually *spreads* or *expands full circle* around the earth or to the *four corners* of the earth.

- **Examples of 4 as related to the earth realm.**

1. We live in *FOUR dimensions* of the natural *earth* realm: Height, Length, Width, and Time.
2. There are *FOUR corners* of the *earth*, as depicted by the main directional designations of a compass: North, East, South, and West.

REVELATION 20:8
and will go out to deceive the nations in the **four corners** of the **earth** [Bold type added]

3. We most commonly consider there to be *FOUR seasons* in a year as the *Earth*

comes *full circle* around the sun: winter, spring, summer, and fall.

- **4 starts in one place and then spreads around the earth**

EXAMPLES:

1. **There are *FOUR* Gospels to be spread *fully around* the world or to the *four corners of the earth*. Matthew, Mark, Luke, and John.**

MARK 16
THE GREAT COMMISSION
And He said to them, "**Go into *all the world*** and preach **the gospel** to every creature. He who believes and is baptized will be saved; but he who does not believe will be condemned. [Bold type and Italics added]

MATTHEW 24
And this gospel of the kingdom will be preached in **all the world** as a witness to all the nations, **and then the end will come.** [Bold type added]

2. **The FOUR Horsemen of the Apocalypse**

One of the reasons there are *four* horsemen is to symbolize that these spirits of destruction will *spread out* to afflict the *entire earth*. Their destruction will be a *worldwide* event.

3. FOUR angels bound at the Euphrates River

These *four angels* will be released at a future appointed time. This event is an example of the number 4 being used to depict that concept of an event that is *initiated in one location*, the Euphrates River, and then *spreads* around to the 4 corners of the *earth*. In 2003, you may have been quite uneasy in your spirit about the long-term effects of the US invasion of Iraq. Now in 2015, with the rise of ISIS, your uneasiness may be increased. The Euphrates River flows through Turkey, Syria, and Iraq. It looks likely that events occurring around the Euphrates River will spiritually lead to spreading worldwide conflict and to our next world war: WWIII. It is possible that the initial invasion of Iraq started a chain of events that "activated" the following Scripture.

REVELATION 9: 13–15 (NKJV)
SIXTH TRUMPET: THE ANGELS FROM THE EUPHRATES
Then the sixth angel sounded: And I heard a voice from the **four horns** of the golden altar which is before God, saying to the sixth angel who had the trumpet, *"Release the four angels who are bound at the great river Euphrates."* So the **four** angels, who had been prepared for the hour and day and month and year, *were released*

to kill a third of mankind. [Bold type and Italics added]

If you have previously read this Scripture, did you ever stop to wonder why God mentioned that He has *four* angels bound? Is this a coincidence or is He foreshadowing a worldwide event, which is consistent with His use of the number 4? He could have bound 7 or 10 or whatever number of angels. God's intentional binding of exactly *four* angels illustrates His consistency in using numbers.

One-third of mankind today is approximately 2.5 billion people. This is how many people will be killed in this world war if this war occurs over the next few years.

Because the *spiritual effects* of the angels' release are to spread to the 4 corners of the earth, the first official shots of WWIII do not necessarily have to *physically* start in the general vicinity of the Euphrates River. It could physically start anywhere in the world. For example, this physical war could start between China and the USA.

The United States' invasion of Iraq spiritually shook up many nations around the world. It initiated a string of reactions and undesirable events that has had worldwide implications. This includes reactions from China. Since 2003, we have seen China's military buildup increase at an alarming rate. We have seen them provocatively test our military in the open seas, in the air, and now in space with their focus on developing capabilities to destroy orbiting satellites. Their cyber-attacks on the USA have also greatly increased in number and in seriousness. So, although today it seems likely that WWIII could physically emanate from the area of the Euphrates River, where ISIS, Russia, the USA and others are fighting, keep an open mind that the first physical shots of WWIII could emanate between China and the USA. It might be wise to keep your eye out for any rise in tensions between these two nations.

CHAPTER 19

THE NUMBER FORTY (40)

The number 40 may be the second number most widely recognized by readers of the Bible. The number 7 is probably the foremost recognized number. God uses the number 40 to represent *a time of trial and/or testing that leads to a new birth or a new beginning*. New beginnings associated with the number 40 start new eras, which do not last forever. They end with the start of yet another new era. In this respect, new beginnings associated with the number 40 are often *cyclical* in nature.

It is important to *distinguish* this number from the number 8, because the number 8 also has a component of a new beginning. I will describe this distinction later in the next chapter.

Here are a few examples of the number 40 in the Bible:

- It rained *40 days* and *40 nights* when God flooded the Earth at the time of Noah and his ark. This was a time of trial that ended in a new beginning for the inhabitants of the ark. It was the start of their lives on the post-flood land.

- The Israelites sent spies into the Promised Land for *40 days*. In this instance, they *failed* to pass the test.

NUMBERS 14:34
ISRAEL REFUSES TO ENTER CANAAN
According to the number of the days in which you spied out the land, *forty days*, a year for each day, you shall bear your iniquity *forty years*, and you shall know my displeasure. [Bold type and Italics added]

The 40-day time of testing ended in failure. Its end marked the start of a new era associated with a number 40. The *40-day* time of testing was extended to a *40-year* time of testing. As such, the Israelites remained in the desert wilderness for 40 years. This, in turn, was a time of trial and testing that led to the subsequent new beginning of their entry into their Promised Land.

- Moses was on Mount Sinai for *40 days* fasting before God gave him the Ten Commandments.

- Yeshua was in the desert for *40 days* being tempted by Satan prior to the new beginning of His ministry.

- Yeshua appeared to witnesses for *40 days* after His resurrection. This was a test of faith not only for the eyewitnesses, but even more so for those who did not see Him with their own eyes during those 40 days, such as you and I. The new beginning associated with this 40 was His ascension into heaven.

JOHN 20:29 (NKJV)
Jesus said to him, "Thomas, because you have seen Me, you have believed. Blessed *are* those who have not seen and *yet* have believed."

Here is a perfect example of the number 40 seen commonly today:

- The pregnancy term for a human is *40 weeks*. This is perfectly consistent with how God uses the number 40 as this represents *a time of trial that ends in a new birth and beginning.*

CHAPTER 20

THE NUMBER EIGHT (8)

God also uses the number 8 to symbolize *a new beginning*. Therefore, *both* numbers 8 and 40 represent a new beginning. However, unlike the new beginning associated with the number 40 that has an endpoint, a new beginning associated with the number 8 is one *that will last for all eternity*. There will be no subsequent new beginning to follow.

In the beginning of 2008, many in the Christian church were describing the number 8 as the number that God uses to symbolize new beginnings and were talking about new beginnings that might occur that year. But when they were talking about their hopes for a new beginning, I always asked, "What *kind* of new beginning?" In my opinion, you will gain additional clarity and understanding from Scripture if you know to distinguish the new beginning of a 40 from a new beginning of an 8.

Here are some examples of the number 8 as used in the Bible to represent a new beginning that will last for eternity.

- **The covenant that God made with Abraham is everlasting; one that will last for eternity.**

GENESIS 17:7 (NKJV)

And I will establish My covenant between Me and you and your descendants after you in their generations, **for an everlasting covenant**, to be God to you and your descendants after you. [Bold type added]

- **Consistent with the way God often uses the number 8, He mandates the use of the number in *the sign of this covenant*.**

The physical sign of circumcision of all males on the *eighth* day of life is the spiritual representation of this *everlasting* covenant.

GENESIS 17:10–13 (NKJV)

This *is* My covenant which you shall keep, between Me and you and your descendants after you: Every male child among you shall be circumcised; and you shall be circumcised in the flesh of your foreskins, **and it shall be a sign of the covenant between Me and you. For the generations to come** every male among you who is **eight days old** must be circumcised, including those born in your household or bought with money from a foreigner – those who are not your offspring. Whether born in your household or bought with your money, they must be circumcised. My covenant in your flesh is to be an *everlasting* covenant. [Bold type and Italics added]

Even many of my Jewish friends do not know that God's commandment for physical circumcision is a sign of the *eternal* spiritual covenant between Abraham and all his descendants. Fewer yet know the symbolic numerical reason why God commanded them to perform it on the *eighth day*. Ultimately, the physical act of circumcision foreshadows the *eternal* covenant that God wants to make with our spiritual hearts.

DEUTERONOMY 30:6 (NKJV)
And the LORD your God will **circumcise your heart** and the heart of your descendants, to love the LORD your God with all your heart and with all your soul, **that you may live.** [Bold type added]

ROMANS 2:29
And *circumcision is a matter of the heart*, by the Spirit, not by the letter. [Bold type and Italics added]

- **Only eight people, including Noah, survived the Great Flood.**

1 PETER 3:20–22 (CJB)
God waited patiently during the building of the ark, in which a few people—to be specific, *eight*—were delivered by means of water. This also prefigures what delivers us now, the water

of immersion, which is not the removal of dirt from the body, but one's pledge to keep a good conscience toward God, through the resurrection of Yeshua the Messiah.

The new beginning that was associated with the 8 people on the ark is one that will last for all eternity. Through these 8 people, the earth was re-populated. Also associated with this use of 8 is the eternal promise never to again destroy the Earth with a flood.

GENESIS 9:11 (NKJV)
Thus I establish My **covenant** with you: **Never again** shall all flesh be cut off by the waters of the flood; **never again** shall there be a flood to destroy the earth." [Bold type added]

- **The start of the 8th millennium will be an era that will last for eternity.**

It has been almost 6,000 years since the time of Adam and Eve. The Bible teaches that failed human government will ultimately lead to near total destruction of all mankind. The next thousand-year period following the approximate 6,000-year period will be the *seventh* millennium, during which time Yeshua, the Christ, will personally and physically rule along with His saints in this earth realm (See Revelation 20:4–6) After the end of this seventh millennium, an *eighth* period will begin. This *eighth* period will not be a millennium, but it will be *a new beginning that will last for all eternity.*

- **It is interesting to note that our modern symbol for infinity resembles the number 8 turned on its side.**

In conclusion, when you see God using the number 8 in the Bible and within the world today, consider that He may be using it not only as a representation of a new beginning, but also *a new beginning that lasts for eternity.*

CHAPTER 21

THE NUMBER FIVE (5)

The number 5 is the number of *God's Grace*. We are saved by grace alone through the Father's gift of Yeshua (whose base number is 2, see Part II, Chapter 32) followed by the gift of His Holy Spirit (3) entering our hearts. This is symbolized in the simple mathematical equation: $2 + 3 = 5$.

Several Biblically significant numbers are associated with The United States of America. The number 5, in the form of 50, is one of these numbers. Fifty is God's grace (5) in a multiple of God's divine order (10). As such, 50 is also numerically symbolic of the grace that God has had on this country. Fifty states comprise the final makeup of The United States of America. The number 50 also represents jubilee. If you study of history of the American Revolution and the War of 1812, the odds of an American victory against the British were miserably poor. This country, which dedicated its foundation to the God of the Bible, was granted *God's grace* to not only become a great nation, but also to play a role in fulfilling His will on this earth. Groups and citizens from this nation have done more to spread the Good News of the Gospel to the four corners of the earth than from any other modern nation in the world today. Grace is the power of God working through us to fulfill His will on earth. For a wonderful Biblical understanding of grace, please web search: "James Ryle definition of grace".

God's Grace for America is contained in the lyrics of *America the Beautiful*.

> O beautiful for spacious skies,
> For amber waves of grain,
> For purple mountain majesties
> Above the fruited plain!
> America! America!
> **God shed His grace on thee,**

In this light, it is no accident that the final makeup of The United States of America consists of 50 states. The historical path of The United States of America could have taken many different turns which could have resulted in the final count of states being different than 50. For example, what if there were only *one* Carolina and/or *one* Dakota; that is, no north or south versions of these states? What if West Virginia hadn't broken off of Virginia at the time of the Civil War? What if the people of northern California had been successful in breaking off from the state of California to create the state of Jefferson? Any of these scenarios and many more could have resulted in a final state count that was a number different than 50. The United States of America did not grow to 50 states through randomness of history. It did so under the grace of God and under His orchestration of history. God has numerically marked the USA with the number 50.

Other numbers associated with the foundation, development, and historical role of The United States of America are also consistent with how God uses numbers in the Bible and in the world around us. These include the number 13 and the pattern of 7/4. Please see also Part II, Chapter 25: *THE NUMBER 13* for more information how The United States of America was numerically labeled at its founding as a *priestly nation*, and Part II, Chapter 31: *THE PATTERN OF 7/4*.

CHAPTER 22

THE NUMBER TEN (10)

The number 10 is associated with *God's divine order*. Only a few examples are presented in this book.

- **The Ten Commandments.**

Although 613 commandments can be counted in the First Testament, God wrote *10* commandments on *2* tablets and gave them to Moses.

- **Humans are made in the image of God.**

The fact that humans are born with *10* fingers and *10* toes is consistent with *God's divine order*.

- **A tithe to the Lord represents 10 percent**

- **The Parable of the Ten Virgins**

MATTHEW 25:1–3
Then the kingdom of heaven will be like **ten** virgins who took their lamps and went to meet the bridegroom. **Five** of them were foolish, and **five** were wise. For when the foolish took their

lamps, they took no oil with them.
[Bold type added]

The Lord offers salvation through grace to *all people*. This offer to all is His intended divine order and, as such, is represented by a total of *10* virgins. Even though it is God's desire for *all* to be saved, only *five* were wise and accepted the salvation of grace made available through Yeshua. As such, only *five* were righteous in God's eyes. Even though grace was also offered to the foolish *five*, they rejected it and will be left out. The number 5 is the number for God's grace as seen in the previous chapter.

CHAPTER 23

THE NUMBER TWELVE (12)

The number 12 is God's number for *wise counsel and / or divine government.*

- **The 12 tribes of Israel came from the 12 sons of Jacob.**

When the Israelites entered their promised land, this land was divided up amongst their tribes into 12 allotments or governmental provinces.

- **Yeshua had 12 disciples.**

Why didn't Yeshua choose a different number of disciples? The 12 chosen represented the start of a Divine Government, despite the later betrayal by Judas.

- **The jury system in the United States of America has 12 members as a hoped for representation of a wise counsel.**

Is it merely a coincidence, in a country dedicated to the God of the Bible at its foundation, that we have 12 members of a jury, which are purposed to represent a *wise counsel?* No!

CHAPTER 24

THE NUMBER ELEVEN (11)

When *a group of people* get together and do something that is *unwise in God's eyes*, a number 11 is often associated with it. Eleven falls short of God's number for wise counsel, divine government, the number 12.

As a reminder, the concept of *numerically falling short* is also seen with the number 6, which represents the efforts of man, falling short of the number 7, which represents a completed act of God in the earth realm (see also Part II, Chapter 16). This same concept is also seen with 9 falling short of 10 (see also Part II, Chapter 27).

Here are a few examples of Biblical *chapter numbers* of 11 that contain themes of unwise actions by groups of people.

If nothing else, the following can serve as a *memory aid* for those who want to remember where to find these stories in the Bible.

NUMBERS 11:1
THE PEOPLE COMPLAIN
And the **people complained** in the hearing of the LORD about their misfortunes, and when

the LORD heard it, his anger was kindled, and the fire of the LORD burned among them and consumed some outlying parts of the camp. [Bold type added]

In this occasion, we can see a group of complaining about God's will for them. This was *not wise* and this angered the LORD.

In Genesis *11* tells of the very first time in the Bible that a group of people got together and attempted something *unwise in the eyes of God*.

GENESIS 11:1–4, 8–9
THE TOWER OF BABEL

Now the whole earth had one language and the same words. And as people migrated from the east, they found a plain in the land of Shinar and settled there. And they said to one another, "Come, let us make bricks, and burn them thoroughly." And they had brick for stone, and bitumen for mortar. Then they said, "Come, let us build ourselves a city and a tower with its top in the heavens, and let us make a name for ourselves, lest we be dispersed over the face of the whole earth." . . . So the LORD dispersed them from there over the face of all the earth, and they left off building the city. Therefore its name was called Babel, because there the LORD confused the language of all the earth. And from there the LORD dispersed them over the face of all the earth.

These people didn't want to be dispersed. God wanted them dispersed. The people did not get their way.

Here is an example in which 11 is used in relationship to a passage of time involving a plot by an unwise group of people.

Eleven months transpired between the date of command and the date of intended execution of the Jews in the kingdom of Persia. The wise council of God prevailed in the *twelfth* month. (The Jewish nation is God's priestly nation. So also note the inclusion of the number 13 in the following text and note that God uses 13 to represent His priests or priestly nations. See also the next chapter in this book on the number 13).

ESTHER 3:12–13
HAMAN'S CONSPIRACY AGAINST THE JEWS
Then the king's scribes were summoned on the **thirteenth** day of the *first* month, and an edict, according to all that Haman commanded, was written to the king's satraps and to the governors over all the provinces and to the officials of all the peoples, to every province in its own script and every people in its own language. It was written in the name of King Ahasuerus and sealed with the king's signet ring. Letters were sent by couriers to all the king's provinces with instruction to destroy, to kill, and to annihilate all Jews, young and old, women and children, in one day, the

thirteenth day of the *twelfth* month, which is
the month of Adar, and to plunder their goods.
[Bold type and Italics added]

But a great reversal in fortune occurred. Haman's
conspiracy was revealed and he was hanged.

ESTHER 7:10
HAMAN IS HANGED

And the king said, "Hang him on that." So
they hanged Haman on the gallows that he had
prepared for Mordecai.

And 11 months later, the Jews destroyed the group
of people who had wanted to destroy them.

ESTHER 9:1–2
THE JEWS DESTROY THEIR ENEMIES

Now in the *twelfth* month, which is the month
of Adar, on the **thirteenth** day of the same,
when the king's command and edict were about
to be carried out, on the very day when the
enemies of the Jews hoped to gain the mastery
over them, the reverse occurred: the Jews
gained mastery over those who hated them.
The Jews gathered in their cities throughout all
the provinces of King Ahasuerus to lay hands
on those who sought their harm. And no
one could stand against them, for the fear of
them had fallen on all peoples. [Bold type and

Italics added]

Examples of 11 possibly representing a group of unwise people in modern-day world

Chapter 11 bankruptcy is one form of bankruptcy in US law. Wise people usually do not go bankrupt if they are dealing with circumstances they can control.

Watch the news for things done by groups of 11 and see if what they are doing would be consistent with foolishness in God's eyes. If you pay attention to this, you will probably see a large number of incidences in which an 11 appears to be numerically marking an *unwise group of people*.

Please see also Part II, Chapter 27, to see how God may have used the number 11 associated with the 9/11 attack on America to foreshadow a warning for a *future unwise group of people*.

CHAPTER 25

THE NUMBER THIRTEEN (13)

The number 13 is God's number for *His priests and for His priestly nations*.

In popular culture 13 is usually associated with a bad or evil number, such as Friday the 13th. This is a common popular misconception. This misconception is perpetuated in modern culture. Elevator control panels in buildings often omit the number 13. Even a major hospital in Dallas perpetuates this misconception by labeling operating rooms with numbers 12 & 12A, instead of 12 & 13. This is nothing but succumbing to *numerology* out of superstition and/or ignorance. In Divine Numerics, 13 is actually a *good* number.

Thirteen is even part of the numerical Fibonacci sequence which numerically illustrates God's consistent design of our material universe from the smallest of things, such as DNA helical structure to the largest, such as the configurations of galaxies. If 13 is associated with God's design of our material universe and God created everything as good, how could 13 represent something evil? The answer is that it does not. But the deception is that, if God uses 13 to represent His priests or His priestly nations, Satan is going to try to turn this around and try to have us believe that 13 is an evil number. Don't fall for this deception.

- **The entire nation of the Israelites was to be a priestly nation.**

EXODUS 19:5–6 (NKJV)
Tell the children of Israel: . . . And you shall be to Me **a kingdom of priests and a holy nation**. [Bold type added]

- **The Levite tribe was the tribe of priests to the other Israelites tribes. The number 13 illustrates the priestly relationship of the Levite tribe to the other tribes with respect to how the Promised Land was divided.**

When the Israelites entered the land promised to them by God, this land was divided up into 12 sections. There were also a total of 12 tribes of Israel. However, two allotments of land were given to the sons of Joseph, Ephraim and Manasseh. This created *13* groups of people. So, one group of people would not be given their own separate allotment of land. The Levite tribe, from which the priests came, was not given an area of land, but rather 4 cities within each of the 12 allotments of land. With this arrangement, they could be *the priests to the other tribes*. As such, in the Promised Land, there were 12 groups of land holding tribes, and the Levitical tribe of priests was the *13th* tribal group to these 12.

- **In the Jewish faith, the age that a man comes into service to God is 13**

We have seen that the entire nation of Israel was to be a priestly nation and that a smaller group, one specific tribe within this nation, the Levites, was to be their tribe of priests. This tribe is associated with a number 13, as described above. Now let's go from nation to smaller tribe down to the individual level. At this level, the number 13 numerically marks transitional age for an individual of the Jewish faith. Today, some might think that this is only keeping with an historic tradition. But it also seems to be consistent with how God uses numbers in our world today. There is a consistent reason why this transitional age occurs at 13 years.

The Jewish celebration of Bar Mitzvah occurs on the *13th* birthday of a male, as he officially becomes a man in service to God; a priest. According to the website Judaism 101, the term Bar Mitzvah technically refers to the child who is coming of age, "Under Jewish Law, children are not obligated to observe the commandments. . . . At the age of 13 (12 for girls), children *become obligated* to observe the commandments."[10]

- **Priests are to aid in the transition of man to God.**

The number 13 can be broken down into 6 + 7 = 13. Priests are to aid in the transition of man (6) to God's work in the earth realm (7).

- **The First Testament of the Christian Bible contains *39 books*.**

The First Testament of the Christian Bible contains *39 books.* The fact that 3 x 13 = 39 can be viewed numerically consistent with The First Testament being fully inspired by the Spirit of God (symbolized by 3) and then given to the priestly nations (symbolized by 13).

- **The number 13 is *not* mentioned in the text of the entire Second Testament.**

The number 13, as represented by the words "thirteen" or "thirteenth," appears in the First Testament text twenty-four times. However, 13 is not mentioned in the text of the entire Second Testament. Perhaps this is because The Second Testament is *all* about the Most High Priest, Yeshua!

Yeshua is our Most High Priest.

HEBREWS 9:11

But Christ came *as **High Priest*** of the good things to come, with the greater and more perfect tabernacle not made with hands, that is, not of this creation. [Bold type and Italics added]

Numerically consistent with His role of High Priest, Yeshua takes on 12 disciples for His divine government. Yeshua is the *13th* to this group of 12.

- **Did you ever wonder if there was a spiritual reason why The United States of America arose out of 13 colonies?**

At its founding, The United States of America was historically and spiritually dedicated to the God of the Bible. Groups and citizens from this nation have done more to spread the good news of the gospel to the four corners of the earth than from any other nation of this Earth. As such, The United States of America has been one of God's *priestly nations* to the world. Numerically consistent with this, the United States of America began with 13 colonies, followed by 13 states. This was not a random act of history. The first flags of The United States contained 13 stars to represent the first 13 states.

The "Betsy Ross" flag, showing the original 13 colonies.

Historically, our land could have started out with a different number colonies and states. What if there had been only *one* Carolina? Or what if some of the *13* colonies did not join into the American Revolution? The number *very easily* could have been different than 13.

CHAPTER 26

THE NUMBER EIGHTEEN (18)

B ased upon the information made available to me, I believe God uses the number 18 to represent *eternal life.*

Several years ago, I was working with one of my Jewish gastroenterologist friends who told me that when they gave money gifts to their children, they were in multiples 18; such as $18, $36 or $180, et cetera. This comes from the fact that the Hebrew word for life, "chai," has two Hebraic letters, which have numerical values of 8 and 10, which add up to 18, 8 + 10 = 18.

The Hebraic word *Chai* (חי) figures prominently in modern Jewish culture, and is often used as a visual symbol. You may see some of your Jewish friends wearing the Chai symbol as a medallion around their neck.

Although many Jewish people wish others long life with their gifts of multiples of 18, God seems to be using 18 to represent *eternal life*. In God's divine order (10), we were created as eternal spiritual beings. His creation of us was our new beginning that will last for all eternity 8. In this sense, $8 + 10 = 18$ may also represent eternal life.

Yeshua died on the cross at the last hours of the 14th day of the Jewish month of Nisan. After 3 full nights and 3 full days (3 is an act of God completed in the spirit realm). He came back to *eternal life*. He first *appeared* to His disciples on the *18th day* of Nisan. This 18 numerically represents the *eternal life* that He has made available to all who accept Him.

Perhaps the future rapture of the church may be associated with a number 18 in some way.

CHAPTER 27

THE NUMBER NINE (9) AND A NUMERICAL INTERPRETATION OF THE 9/11 ATTACK ON AMERICA

God most often uses the number 9 to represent *a judgment*. The verdict or outcome of a judgment can take the form of a blessing or of a curse. Because of their relationship to a judgment, both blessings and curses, in turn, can also be associated with the number 9. A curse can also be associated with *chaos, darkness, and destruction*; all of which *fall short* of God's divine desired order (the number 9 falls short of the number 10). Alternatively, a blessing is associated with many favorable outcomes. Our behavior and choices in life will determine whether we will receive judgments of blessings or of curses.

- The ultimate and final *judgment of and provision for the sins of the world* occurred in the *9th hour* of the day that Yeshua was crucified. All of the sins of mankind, past, present and future were put upon Yeshua. This provision for sin is a blessing to those who will accept and acknowledge what Yeshua has done for them.

LUKE 23:44 (NKJV)
Now it was about the sixth hour, and there was darkness over all the earth until the **ninth hour**. Then the sun was darkened, and the veil of the temple was torn in two. And when Jesus had cried out with a loud voice, He said, "Father, *'into Your hands I commit My spirit.'* Having said this, He breathed His last. [Bold type added]

- In the Hebraic alphabet, the *word picture* associated with the number 9 is *the serpent*, one of the symbols for Satan. Satan, in turn, embodies *chaos, darkness, and destruction.*

- **The 9 fruits and 9 gifts of the Holy Spirit.**

In my Bible study circles, I am often asked if the number 9 is the number of the Holy Spirit. I respond by saying *instead* of saying that 9 is the number of the Holy Spirit, it would be more accurate to say that both the number 9 and the number 3 *have associations* with the Holy Spirit. I then go on to say that the number 9 is more specifically used by God in association with a *judgment*, whereas the number 3 is more specifically associated with the Holy Spirit and completed acts of

God in the spirit realm (see also Part II, Chapter 17). Many then respond by asking, "What about the 9 fruits of the Holy Spirit?" The teaching that there are 9 fruits of the Holy Spirit comes from the following Biblical verse: In this the number 9 is not literally written in the text, but is a simple *enumeration* of characteristics listed in this verse.

> **GALATIANS 5:22–23**
> But the fruit of the Spirit is love, joy, peace, patience, kindness, goodness, faithfulness, gentleness, self-control; against such things there is no law.

On the surface, this might seem to be an assignment by man. One could make an argument that it is *the reader*, who has *counted* the number of fruits listed in this Bible verse, came up with the number 9 and then assigned significance to this number to the Holy Spirit. I have not seen any strong evidence of God literally using the *written* number 9 as an assignment to the Holy Spirit. In this verse, it may be more accurate and consistent with how God is using the number 9 to think of the *9 enumerated fruits* as 9 aspects of our lives upon which *God may judge us.* Here is an important question that we should ask ourselves: If we are truly born again in our spirit by the Spirit of God, do we have any evidence of such fruit in our lives that is consistent with being reborn in our spirit?

In addition to the enumeration of 9 *fruits* of the Holy Spirit, readers of the Bible have also enumerated 9 *gifts* of the Holy Spirit. These are found in 1 Corinthians 12:4–11.

1 CORINTHIANS 12:4–10

Now there are varieties of gifts, but the same Spirit; and there are varieties of service, but the same Lord; and there are varieties of activities, but it is the same God who empowers them all in everyone. To each is given the manifestation of the Spirit for the common good. For to one is given through the Spirit the utterance of wisdom, and to another the utterance of knowledge according to the same Spirit, to another faith by the same Spirit, to another gifts of healing by the one Spirit, to another the working of miracles, to another prophecy, to another the ability to distinguish between spirits, to another various kinds of tongues, to another the interpretation of tongues.

Here again, the actual number 9 is not written in the Biblical text. This verse says that there are a variety of gifts and enumerates 9 categories of them. But just because 9 categories are enumerated in this verse, it doesn't have to mean that there can't be more than 9. If the Bible had said that there are only 9 categories of gifts of the Holy Spirit, then that would definitively be a different story. However, God may still be using the number 9 to represent the blessings of His Holy Spirit.

Is it possible that God uses the number 9 to represent a judgment, chaos, darkness, and destruction on one hand, yet on the other hand to represent an association with the enumerated fruits and gifts of the Holy Spirit? Yes, *both possibilities could be true.* On the surface, these two interpretations of how God uses the number 9 seem to be at odds with each other. But at a deeper level of consideration, one may ask, "If there is a warning of future judgment 9, then what will be the outcome of that judgment? Will the outcome of the judgment be a favorable blessing or an unfavorable curse?"

The answer to this may depend upon how a person or nation responds to a circumstance or event. If a person or nation continues to behave *unwisely* in the eyes of God, 11, the judgment will take the form of a curse against them leading to destruction. If, on the other hand, a person or nation heeds the warning of a pending judgment, the outcome will be favorable in the form of a blessing. If you are judged to be righteous in the eyes of God through your acceptance of Yeshua as both Lord and Savior of your life, then you will also be blessed with the *gifts and fruits of God's Holy Spirit,* which also have been associated with the number 9.

Therefore, God most often uses the number 9 to represent *a judgment.* But He may also use the number 9 in association with the *outcome* of His judgment, which can take the form of either a blessing or a curse.

THE 9TH OF AV

The *9th of Av* is the day in the yearly Jewish calendar that is most associated with catastrophe for the Jewish people. Starting in the year *1313 BC*, more catastrophes have happened to the Jewish nation on this calendar date than on any other day of the year. It was on this day in 1313 BC, during the time of Moses, that God punished the Israelites for not trusting Him. They had refused to enter their Promised Land when He first told them to enter. (Note also the double 13 in the year.) God's *judgment* against them resulted in an extension of their time in the desert to 40 years.

On this same calendar day, their first temple on the Temple Mount in Jerusalem was destroyed in 587 BC by Nebuchadnezzar. Also on this very same calendar day in 70 AD, their Second Temple was destroyed by the Romans! Numerous other catastrophes throughout history occurred on the 9th of Av. Each of these could be viewed as *a judgment* or at least *a reminder of the original judgment* that God placed on the Jewish nation at the time of Moses. The numerous catastrophes for the Jewish people associated with the 9th of Av can be easily found with a simple internet search.

Therefore, much *historical evidence* exists that God has used the number 9 in association with a *judgment*; one that originated with the Israelites' refusal to trust Him, and to enter their Promised Land.

9 US SUPREME COURT JUSTICES

It is interesting that in this nation founded on principles from the Bible, not only do we most commonly have 12 members of a jury in an attempt to represent wise counsel and divine government, but also 9 judges in our Supreme Court, the highest court of the US government. Final legal *judgments* from the judicial branch of government in this country come from here. A nation truly "one nation under God," as stated in the American Pledge of Allegiance, should receive final legal judgments from its Supreme Court that are consistent with God's ways. If we do not receive such consistent judgments, we are "under God" only when it suits the ideology and desires of the Supreme Court Justices. Ultimately, God Almighty will be *the final judge* of the judgments handed down by the American Supreme Court.

A NUMERICAL INTERPRETION OF THE 9/11 ATTACK ON AMERICA

Many have wondered if the terrorist intentionally chose the date September 11, 2001 (9/11) as a symbolic representation of the *911* emergency telephone number used in The United States. This number was established in 1967 by the Federal Communications Commission and AT&T. Whether the terrorist intentionally chose this number or not, God's use of the numbers 9 and 11 would give another meaning to the emergency number.

Simply put, the 9/11 attack on America is *a foreshadowing of judgment (9) of the group of people who are unwise in the eyes of God (11).* Numbers associated with this attack also foreshadow Yeshua's return at Armageddon, at which time judgment will occur.

Note also that both numbers 9 and 11 can *numerically fall short* of God's desire for the earth. If the verdict of a judgment is negative, 9 will manifest in destruction; this falls short of 10, God's desired divine order. 11, an unwise group, falls short of 12, wise counsel.

God's numerical labeling the 9/11 attack as a portent of future judgment against the unwise, did not apply to the victims of the tragedy. This was not a judgment against them. They were innocent victims. Any possible foreshadowing and warning, instead, are meant for those of us still alive. God did not perpetrate the evil of these attacks. But God will still turn things around and use evil for His good. If the terrorist hijackers actively chose the date of 9/11 to represent the 911 telephone system 3-digit emergency code, God would apply *His* meaning to these same numbers for His good. And His good is meant for our good: This warning is meant for our benefit.

Many have described the events of 9/11 as a wakeup call for America. The attacks on the World Trade Center in New York City and on the Pentagon building in Washington, on this day were tragic events. You may or may not recall that in the weeks that followed the 9/11 attack, it seemed like almost everyone was patriotically proclaiming "God bless America!" Not only was this proclaimed verbally, but also on roadside billboards and signs in open fields. Billboards and signs popped up just about everywhere. In addition, the churches were packed.

It is selfish and ignorantly reckless for some people to proclaim "God bless America!" when they want God to do something for them, but at other times, these same people say, "God, get out of our schools, get out of our courts, remove your Ten Commandment monuments and crosses from our public lands, and get out of our social morality! We will call you only when we need you." You can't put God in an emergency box and break the glass only when you think you need Him! Biblical history has shown that He will not put up with such mindsets for long.

The attack of 9/11 was a spiritual wakeup call for me that initiated the process of obtaining the information for this book. Indeed, this event was a spiritual wakeup call for many at that time. But since then, only a minority of people has remained awake spiritually. Most people have gone back to sleep spiritually. The only thing that might remain awake in these people is an awareness of the *earthly* potential dangers of the radical jihadists. They have gone back to living exclusively inside their 4-dimensional bubble. (See Part I, Chapter 8.) These people are unaware that something much bigger than what is confined to our 4th dimension may be occurring.

In truth, the 9/11 attack on America was more than a temporary patriotic wakeup call. It was foremost a spiritual *warning* to repent as a nation and turn back to the God of the Bible. This warning can be seen through the examination of specific parallels between historical events found in the Bible and the 9/11 attack. This warning can also be seen through an understanding of God's numerical marking of the 9/11 event. In addition to being a warning, the 9/11 attack was also a symbolic foreshadowing of Yeshua's return at Armageddon. I will offer substantive evidence of this assertion later in this book.

The specific parallels between historical events found in the Bible and the 9/11 attack, God's warning to America, has been clearly documented by Rabbi Jonathan Cahn in his book, *The Harbinger*, and DVD, *The Isaiah 9:10 Judgment*.[11] If you have not read or seen this information, I would highly recommend that you do so, as it shows that God is clearly active in orchestrating specific realities in our world today for the purpose of communicating to those who would open their hearts to Him. In his book and video, Rabbi Cahn identifies very specific, uncanny parallels between the historical attack by the Syrians on the Northern Kingdom of Israel in 732 BC and the 9/11 attacks on America.

In addition to these specific parallels, Rabbi Cahn points out that two extremely prominent American politicians even quoted the Isaiah 9:10 Scripture in formal speeches. But they quoted Isaiah 9:10 fully *out of context*. They did not convey the context of the verses before or after the specific verse of Isaiah 9:10. The full context of Isaiah 9 chapter is a *judgment against a nation* that remained proud and arrogant after an initial attack by an enemy and did not turn back to God. Both of these politicians no longer hold national political office. Their names are former Senate Majority Leader Tom Daschle and former Presidential candidate John Edwards.

From a numerical perspective, it is interesting that Rabbi Cahn has identified a total of 9 harbingers that portend judgment in the parallels between the destroyed Kingdom of Northern Israel and the 9/11 attack. This is fully consistent with God's use of the number 9 to represent *judgment*.

One can find numerous other numerical associations between the 9/11 attack. For example, many have noted that New York State is America's *11th* state. Also, American Airlines Flight number *11* was the first plane to crash into the World Trade Center towers. Henry Hudson, the explorer after whom the Hudson River was named, first anchored at Manhattan on **9/11**/1609.[12] Some have also noted that President George H. W. Bush gave his "New World Order" speech to the nation on **9/11**/1990, exactly *11 years* prior to **9/11**/2001.

The twin towers even looked like the number 11.

I have also made the following observation. The twin towers fell down on *9/11* (September 11, 2001) and, with the numbers in reverse order, the Berlin Wall fell on *11/9* (November 9, 1989). Both marked the reality of *a new world order.* The time interval between these events is approximately *11.9 years.*

Because the founders of this nation dedicated this country to the God of the Bible, this country has been blessed and protected in the past. George Mason, a founding father who is also referred to as the father of the US Bill of Rights, reminded the writers of this said document just before the US Constitution was written that as *individuals* we will all be judged by God *after death*. But *nations* do not exist in heaven. There will be no United States of America in heaven. Just as the nation of Israel would experience blessings or curses depending on their alignment with the ways of God, as described in the book of Deuteronomy Chapter 28, so would be the fate of The United States of America. Because Mason understood this reality of God's design, he advocated that the constitution of this nation be written in a way that the nation would receive the blessings of God and avoid His judgments. This is the spiritual reason behind our nation's great historical prosperity.

Tragically, despite the warning of the 9/11 attack, this country has continued to undergo a rapidly progressive separation from God. If this country continues to refuse to repent and continues to force God out of its laws and moral tenets, then God will not continue to bless and protect this nation from evil and its enemies. America will suffer severe devastation.

In light of the fact that 2016 will open the season for World War III, now is the absolute worse time to fall away from God and His protection. We may be left fully vulnerable to our enemies both from financial and military perspectives.

One major event that happened to the Northern Kingdom of Israel has not yet become a parallel event to an event in America. The Syrians attacked the Northern Kingdom of Israel a second time in 722 BC, which was 10 years after their first attack. The first attack had only breached the Kingdom's outer defenses. But the Israelites responded with arrogance and did not turn back to God. The second attack completely destroyed the Northern Kingdom. A parallel of the second attack on the Northern Kingdom of Israel to a future event in America is an ominous prospect.

In addition to the specific historical parallels identified by Rabbi Jonathan Cahn, substantial numerical evidence supports the interpretation that God has used the numbers of 9/11 as a warning to America to *foreshadow a future judgment (9) of the group of people who are unwise in the eyes of God (11).* Unfortunately, even those who have kept wisdom in the eyes of God will also be hit.

CHAPTER 28

THE NUMBER NINETEEN (19)

In a similar numerical format to the number 18 (8 + 10 = 18), God may be using the number 19, 9 + 10 = 19, to represent or foreshadow *the FINAL judgment of all humanity*, as 9 is a judgment in 10 in God's divine order. God's divine order will not be established in this earth realm until He returns and establishes His Kingdom on the Earth.

God's divine order on Earth will be free from sin. As a part of His divine order, He will judge everyone for choices he or she has made during his or her life on earth. This judgment will occur *after* His return to our earth realm. As such, God may be using the number 19 to represent a final judgment of humanity, or a foreshadowing thereof.

Within all the numerical symbolism contained in the 9/11 attack on America, I found it interesting that there were 19 terrorist hijackers. Did this number also foreshadow a final judgment for America? One day, God may let us know the answer to the question.

In our current age of falling away from God, I found the following report consistent with how God uses the number 19. I was watching FOX News one day in early 2015 and I saw a report on the current state of the Bible. Of people surveyed 19 were skeptics and 19 were believers.

This information came from a survey by the Barna Group.[13] In their report, they found that *both* groups, on opposite extremes of belief in Bible validity, represent **19 percent** of the survey sample.

BIBLE LOVERS AND BIBLE SKEPTICS

19% ENGAGED* | **19% SKEPTICAL†**

* Engaged people read the Bible at least 4 times a week and believe that it is the actual or inspired Wo

† People categorized as "skeptics" are those who, from five options, selected the most negative or nor view of the Bible, saying they believe "the Bible is just another book of teachings written by men that contains stories and advice."

I had already come across other evidence that suggested God may be using the number 19 to foreshadow the FINAL judgment of humanity when I saw the report of the Barna Group survey. Because of this prior understanding, their report of *19 percent* really stood out. The result of 19 *percent* represents another piece of numerical evidence that supports the hypothesis that we indeed are living in the last days of human government leading up to God's final judgment.

God's use of the number 19 as a representation or a foreshadowing of the FINAL judgment of all humanity may also point to *the year 2019* as a significant year associated with His return. In fact, the years 2019 and 2020 are the years during which a major Biblically significant numerical convergence will occur. This convergence will be discussed further in Part III.

CHAPTER 29

THE PATTERN OF 7/4 AND THE USA IN THE BIBLE

O ver thirty years ago, my friend Irvin Baxter, Jr., Biblical scholar, founder and president of Endtime Ministries, discovered that the United States was represented symbolically in the Bible. Within the book of Daniel, Irvin noted that there is a lion that had eagle's wings and that, in a prophetic dream, Daniel watched the eagle's wings being plucked off the back of the lion and a heart of a man was given to it.

DANIEL 7:4
The first *was* like a lion, and had eagle's wings. I watched till its wings were *plucked off*, and it was lifted up from the earth and made to stand on two feet like a man, and a man's heart was given to it.

Irvin noted that the major nation in the world today symbolized by the lion is Great Britain; the British Lion. He also noted that the major nation on the earth today symbolized by the eagle is the United States of America.

Since the USA came out of Britain, he has concluded that the act of plucking of the eagle's wings from the back of the lion was God foretelling the world that the nation of the eagle, (USA) would be born out of the nation of the lion (Great Britain).

One day in 2004, I was re-watching Irvin's teaching video of The United States of America found in the Bible. I had seen it several times prior. This time, however, when Daniel 7:4 was shown on the television screen, the numbers *7:4* stood out prominently to me. I froze the video image on the screen and yelled out to my wife, who was in another room of my house, "Tawana! Come in here! You need to see this!" My wife came into the room, took one look at the frozen video image and said, "So what? We've both seen this video before." I responded, "No! Don't you see the numbers?!" She said, "No." I explained, "Irvin is teaching that Daniel symbolically saw in his prophetic dream the signing of the American Declaration of Independence, as represented by the eagle's wings being plucked out of the back of the lion. This event occurred on *July 4*, or *7/4*! So the chapter and verse number placement confirms his interpretation of the Biblical word text!!"

Excited about this observation, I wanted to tell Irvin. So some time shortly thereafter I phoned into his live on air radio program. The conservation went something like this: "So, Irvin. Where in the Bible did Daniel see the signing of the American Declaration of Independence?" Irvin responded, "That is found in Daniel Chapter 7, verse 4." He then continued to explain this further for the radio listening audience.

After his explanation I said something like this, "So it's *not* found in Daniel 7:1 or 7:5 or some other chapter in the book of Daniel. And you see the numbers 7 and 4 are like Independence Day, right?" I don't recall Irvin's exact response, but I ended the conservation with the belief that I was successful in sharing the information with Irvin and his radio audience.

About a year later, my wife and I were sitting in Irvin's office talking with him and with his wife, Judy. I started talking about Biblical numbers and said, "Do you remember the time I called your radio program and pointed out that the chapter and verse numbers of Daniel 7:4 was a numerical confirmation that your interpretation was a correct one? That Daniel foresaw over 2,000 years ahead of time America breaking away from Great Britain?" Irvin paused and looked at his wife, then said he really didn't pick up on what I was trying to say on that phone call, but now both he and Judy understood. So I was happy that I had the opportunity to successfully share this numerical observation with them.

Irvin then asked me if I understood the significance of the 1,335 days in the Daniel chapter 12. He said that he had asked many people about that number and that no one was able to give him an interpretation that seemed valid. I said, "Hmmm . . . I don't understand this number either. But maybe God will let me know what it means someday in the future." Approximately ten years after this conversation, God may have given me the insight to understand the significance of these 1,335 days. I will share this with you in Part III, Chapter 40.

Below, I have combined Irvin's symbolic interpretations with my numerical interpretation and have added these within the Daniel 7:4 Scripture. These interpretations are within [brackets].

DANIEL 7:4

The first *was* like a lion **[Great Britain]**, and had eagle's wings **[The United States of America]**. I watched till its wings were *plucked off* **[The signing of the Declaration of Independence]**; and it was lifted up from the earth **[it was given God's Blessing]** and made to stand on two feet like a man, and a man's heart was given to it **[Uncle Sam, the other symbol of the United States of America]**.

The Great Seal of the United States   Uncle Sam

The British Lion

In addition to looking at how the chapter and verse numbers of Daniel 7:4 seem to confirm the Biblical text interpretation that the Eagle represents The United States of America, let's look to see if the actual way God uses the numbers 7 and 4 is consistent with the historical role that this country has played in this world since its founding.

Why was The United States of America founded in July, the 7th month?

God typically uses the number 7 to represent His completed act in the *earth* realm (in contrast to the number 3, which represents a completed act of God in the *spiritual* realm). The predominant reason why people left the relatively civilized world of Europe for the barely civilized new world was for the opportunity to have religious freedom from the established religious institution in Europe. Many viewed the crossing of the Atlantic Ocean to the new land as symbolic of the crossing of the Red Sea by Moses and the Israelites into their promised land. In fact, the First Great Seal Committee of The United States of America, in July and August of 1776, considered several designs; two of which contained allegoric scenes of Moses and the children of Israel.

> **Benjamin Franklin** suggested "Moses standing on the Shore, and extending his Hand over the Sea, thereby causing the same to overwhelm Pharaoh who is sitting in an open Chariot, a Crown on his Head and a Sword in his Hand. Rays from a Pillar of Fire in the Clouds reaching to Moses, to express that he acts by Command of the Deity. Motto, Rebellion to Tyrants is Obedience to God."

> **Thomas Jefferson** suggested "The children of Israel in the wilderness, led by a cloud by day and a pillar of fire by night . . ."[14]

No evidence can be seen within the design proposals of these two prominent founding fathers that they intended to have a country separate from the God of Bible!

It is clear to me that the success of the American Revolution against the British was an act of God in the earth realm. Our founding fathers dedicated our country's foundation to the God of the Bible. The odds were overwhelming against an American victory, yet they won. It is, therefore, numerically befitting that the month of our nation's birth was in the *7th* month, July.

Why was The United States of America founded on the *4th day* of July?

The specific day in July that the Declaration of Independence was signed was the *4th*. The choice of the 4th is also consistent with how God commonly uses numbers.

There are *two different ways* to interpret God's possible use of the number 4 to mark the day on which America was born. Both ways make sense and add rich illustration of God's numerical consistency.

1. 4 is used to represent the *new birth* of the nation.

The United States of America was born on the 4th of July, 1776. Most people celebrate the anniversary of this event every year. God uses the number 40 to represent a time of trial and ends in a *new birth* or beginning. How does the new birth associated with the number 40 fit into a new birth associated with the number 4? Simply, it is important to learn that God often uses numbers multiplied by factor of 10, yielding larger numbers, or going the other way yielding smaller numbers if multiplied by a fraction of 10, such as 0.1. In this case, 40 x 0.1 = 4. In this light, the number 4 can still be consistent with a new birth, which more commonly associated with the number 40. In addition to this, more *pragmatically*, there is no *July 40th*!

2. 4 starts in one place and then spreads around the earth.

The second way the 4th of July is consistent with God's use of the number 4 is that effects of what starts in one place in the world later spreads to have worldwide impact upon the rest of the world. This use of the number 4 was described in Part II, Chapter 18 of this book. Realize that the impact of what *started* that 4th day of July in Philadelphia eventually *spread* to the *4 corners* of the *earth*. History has already recorded the significant impact that The United States of America has had upon the entire world. This impact has been both physical and spiritual.

In conclusion, the founding of The United States of America on July 4, 1776 is consistent with God's use of numbers 7 and 4. This numerical consistency, along with Scripture of Daniel *7:4* and with the history of the country, gives credence to the assertion that the birth of America (4) was an act of God in the earthly realm (7). This in turn, gives more credence to the assertion that The United States of America was also numerically labeled to be a priestly nation of God, as marked by its original 13 states and its growth to 50 states as consistent with God's grace. (See also Part II, Chapters 21 and 25 of this book.)

CHAPTER 30

THE NUMBER FIFTY-TWO (52) – A BIBLICAL GENERATION?

Generations are cyclical in nature. Many of you may be familiar with the term "life cycle" used in biology. As one generation passes through time, it gives life to and is eventually replaced by the next generation. The average life span of human generation has changed throughout human history. It has been affected by war, disease, economic conditions and technology to name a few. So the numbers of years contained within a *biological human generation has varied*.

But is a *biological human generation* different from a *Biblical generation*? If they are different, are they *qualitatively* different, *quantitatively* different, or *both*? How many years quantitatively define a Biblical generation? Unlike that of a biological human generation that has *varied* in length throughout human history, has the number of years in a Biblical generation remained *constant* throughout human history? If so, is this number of years in a Biblical generation also a number that is consistent with how God uses numbers in the Bible and in the world around us today? Moreover, why might this even be important for you to know? This chapter may help in answering these questions.

Among people who study Bible prophecy, there has been confusion and disagreement with regard to how many years are in a Biblical generation. And historically, it has been a moot point of speculation. It really hasn't affected our lives at all. Still, many who study Bible prophecy have speculated that 40 or 70 years represents the correct number. The preponderance of evidence presented in this book suggests that the correct number is about *52 years*. But before we examine the evidence supporting 52, we need to know *why* anyone should even care what the correct number is.

Please recall that in Part I, Chapter 13: DISPELLING THE COMMON TEACHING THAT NO ONE WILL EVER KNOW WHEN CHRIST WILL RETURN lays out compelling arguments why it may be possible that God may let some in the last generation know approximately when Yeshua may return to Earth; perhaps even within a time window of days. In that chapter, I also noted that as human beings we have a natural tendency to want to know *when* something is going to happen. I also gave examples of the prophet Daniel and Yeshua's disciples asking *when* God's kingdom on Earth would be established. So, one of the reasons why people care about the length of a Biblical generation comes from their desire to know approximately when Yeshua will return to the Earth.

In the passage below, Yeshua gives a parable referring to the *season of time*, during which He will return.

MATTHEW 24:32–35

"From the fig tree learn its lesson: as soon as its branch becomes tender and puts out its leaves, you know that summer is near. So also, when you see all these things, you know that he is near, at the very gates. Truly, I say to you, ***this generation will not pass away until all these things take place.*** Heaven and earth will pass away, but my words will not pass away. [Bold type and Italics added]

This fig tree parable informs us that a specific generation is supposed to know *the season* of His return. We have overwhelming evidence that is both amassing and converging to indicate with high probability that we are now living in the correct season. But has God given us *more* specific information to help us to understand when He will return within a *narrower window of time* than just the more vague terms of "some *season* in some future year"? He has, because He has chosen to add the fact that "*this generation will not pass away*" in the above Biblical passage.

With this being true, the next logical questions are: Has God given us clues as to *how many years are in a Biblical generation* that by no means will pass away? Is He using Biblical numbers to give us the answer? If we can answer these questions with some certainty, then the next logical question after that becomes: From *what year* do we *start* counting forward? If He also gives us the year that the last Biblical generation started, then we could simply add to this year the number of years in a Biblical generation to yield an answer of some particular year in the future. Because this generation cannot pass away, this mathematical answer would give us *the absolute latest year* that Christ would physically return to the earth realm. He could, of course, return at any time *before* this generation ends, because He says He will return *before* that generation passes away.

Therefore, some people want to know how many years quantitatively define a *Biblical generation*, because it could be a clue in the puzzle to help answer the question of when Yeshua will return to earth.

To date, most people who study Bible prophecy have focused only on what *quantifies* a Biblical generation. At this point, I would also like to lay out an argument concerning the characteristics that *qualitatively* defines a Biblical generation and how these characteristics *should be consistent with the number* that it contains.

A Biblical generation *qualitatively* includes *a cyclical nature* and *an association with sin*. Because generations are cyclical, as mentioned previously in this chapter, the number that defines a Biblical generation should also have a cyclical character to it.

Because sin is inherent to all generations, the number associated with a Biblical generation should *not* be a number associated with a completed act of God, such as derivatives of the numbers 3 or 7. No completed act of God contains sin.

The argument that a Biblical generation is qualitatively associated with sin is supported by the fact that the Bible specifically talks about the effects of sin being passed down through generations. Sins of one generation have a ripple effect upon subsequent generations. For example, consider the effect of national financial mismanagement and debt by one generation on subsequent generations. You may have also heard of the term "the sins of the father."

EXODUS 34
The LORD passed before him and proclaimed, "The LORD, the LORD, a God merciful and gracious, slow to anger, and abounding in steadfast love and faithfulness, keeping steadfast love for thousands, forgiving iniquity and transgression and sin, but who will by no means clear the guilty, *visiting the iniquity of the fathers on the children and the children's children, to the third and the fourth generation*." [Bold type and Italics added]

Next, I will lay out arguments that support the assertion that 52 years most likely approximates a Biblical generation. After that, I will explain why the numbers 40 and 70 are less likely to be correct, based upon how God most commonly uses numbers in the Bible and based upon the assertion that the arguments supporting number 52 is significantly stronger than the arguments supporting the numbers 40 and 70. All assertions concerning the number of years in a Biblical generation are speculative interpretations. We will not get a definitive truth on this subject until we see the actual event of the abomination of desolation described in the Bible.

Five points suggesting that 52 years most likely quantitatively defines a Biblical generation:

1. 52 weeks in a year is a model seen in God's creation.

Because generations are cyclical, we want to look for evidence that a number has *a cyclical nature* to it. Because God ordained that there be *7 days in a week*, the amount of time it takes for the Earth to revolve around the sun or to come around *full circle* is a year or *52 weeks*. So we have an established sign from God's creation suggesting an association between the concept of coming *full circle* and the number 52. But this model of God's creation is in *weeks*, not years. So now let's look for evidence that this same cyclical concept may also have been established by God on the basis of *years*.

2. The mathematical and symbolic relationship between the numbers 4, 13, and 52.

There is a simple mathematical relationship involving the numbers 4 and 13 that symbolizes a season of time or cycle of God's priestly nation. This is $13 \times 4 = 52$.

Remember that God often uses the number 4 to represent something that comes around full circle, as in four seasons in the year, or that is spread to the 4 corners of the earth. Please also recall that God uses the number 13 numerically to symbolize a priest or a priestly nation. In the Jewish faith, remember that a man officially comes of age in service to God at the age of 13 years. In this sense, 13 years is also the age of accountability to God.

Therefore, the time it takes for a 13–year-old member of the priestly nation to go full circle 4 in his life is 52 years, 13 x 4 = 52. As such, this mathematical equation is a symbolic and conceptual representation of a Biblical generation: 52 years.

3. 52-year intervals are found in The United States seasons for war

The full illustration of the seasons for war in The United States of America will be presented later in this book, Part III, Chapter 2. I mention this topic now, however, because war seasons historically have occurred every *52 years* in the USA. In this world, the natural, sinful nature of humanity has never changed. It appears factual that *every generation has its war*. The reality that wars occur in seasons is even described in the Bible (Ecclesiastes, Chapter 3). Every generation has its sins, and many of these sins are passed down within the circle of life to the following generation.

Remember that the USA was founded as a priestly nation to the God of the Bible. As such, the simple mathematical equation, 13 x 4 = 52, is again applicable. The fact that war cycles occur at *52-year* intervals in the USA is also consistent with *all the other* arguments presented in this chapter that 52 years represents of a *Biblical generation*.

4. Calculations by Dr. Jack Van Impe

Dr. Jack Van Impe, has calculated the number of years in a Biblical generation from information *found in Biblical Scripture.* Based on two different, but similar, calculations, he came up with *51.5* years and *51.9* years. These numbers most closely round up to 52 years.

I received an email in 2004 from his ministries confirming one of the methodologies he used in his calculations. The following is an excerpt from this email:

> "According to Matthew 1:17, there were 42 generations between Abraham and Jesus Christ. This covers a period of 2,160 years. Divide the 2,160 by 42 and it comes to 51.5 years for a generation. Jack Van Impe Ministries"

5. The *77 Mathematical Equation*

The *77 Mathematical Equation* describes a relationship between the number 51.948 and a profound numerical marking for the return of Yeshua to the earth realm, 77. Note that 51.948 rounded up to two-digits = 52. The *77 Mathematical Equation* will be discussed fully in Part II, Chapter 33: *TWO SEVENS* (TWO 7S) – HOW THE LORD APPEARS TO BE USING TWO SEVENS. But the specific point I want to make in this chapter is that, the two-digit number 52 is *again* associated with the return of Yeshua. As such, it is the best numerical candidate to represent the generation that *"will by no means pass away"* before His return.

Whether *the precise number* of years in a Biblical generation is 52 or 51.5 or 51.9 as suggested by Dr. Jack Van Impe or 51.948 years as suggested by the *77 Mathematical Equation*, the conclusion remains the same. Based upon multiple clues, a Biblical generation appears to be approximately *52 years*.

Now let's look at why the numbers 40 and 70 are *less likely* to be correct based upon how God most commonly uses numbers in the Bible.

- **A Biblical generation? 40 years refuted, 52 years supported:**
  A re-examination of conclusions drawn from the 40-year time frame between the exodus from Egypt and entering the Promised Land

Many in the Christian church have described a Biblical generation as 40 years. Much of this thinking stems from that fact that the Israelites spent a total of 40 years in the desert. But the number 40 is a time of trial or testing that ends in some sort of new beginning or a new birth that does not last for an eternity. This was discussed fully in Part II, Chapter 19: THE NUMBER FORTY (40). Forty does have cyclical characteristics associated with it. But, we really need to look more closely at what happened when God extended the Israelite's time in the desert to 40 years.

If you examine Scripture closely, you will see that this extension of time to 40 years was based upon the number of years it would take for those, *whom God held accountable* for refusing to enter the Promised Land, to die out. Those accountable were fighting men of minimum age of *20 years old*. Therefore, the oldest anyone of these men could have been before they died was 60 years old, 20 + 40 = 60. So if people are going to use this Biblical story as a basis to claim how long a Biblical generation is, then they better make their answer 60 years, not 40 years!

Note also, this group was only fighting men. They didn't trust God because they were afraid they would lose their lives in battle. God held this group of people accountable and they had to die before *the rest of Israel* could enter the Promised Land. Accountability was *not* applied to the non-fighting men, who were not in danger of losing their lives in battle, such as the men 13 to 19 years old. Accountability was also *not* applied to any of the children 0 to 12 years old, to those of the priestly tribe of Levi, nor any women of all ages. Any one of these, regardless of their age, could have walked into the Promised Land 40 years later.

If we can use the story of the Israelites' punishment of 40 years in the desert as a conceptual model to figure out how many years are in a Biblical generation, we should really focus on *what age* God *generally* holds people *accountable* for their behavior. That age would apply to *all* competent members of a generation, not just to those who were fighting men. In the specific story of the Exodus, the minimum age of accountability for fighting men was 20 years. But in general, remember that in the Jewish faith a man officially comes of age in service to God at age of 13 years. In that sense, 13 years is also the general age of accountability to God. Therefore, we use age *13* years as the starting point to draw a conclusion that would be applicable to *all members* of a generation.

Well, look what we get when we consider the age of general accountability to be 13. If you are even just one-day shy of your 13th birthday, you are still 12 years old if you count by only whole numbers. Now add 40 years to this number. You get 12 + 40 = 52.

Therefore, when you closely examine the assertion that the story of the Israelites' wanderings' extending to 40 years in the desert can be used as a basis to determine how many years are in a Biblical generation, you find that 40 years would be an inaccurate conclusion, because it would not be applicable to *all* competent members of a generation. The number that would be applicable to all competent members would be *52 years*. And this number, as you already know, is consistent with all of the other arguments supporting 52 years as the correct number contained in a Biblical generation.

- **A Biblical generation? 70 years versus 52 years**

Many who study Bible prophecy have also described a Biblical generation as 70 years. Given the weight of the evidence above supporting 52 years, the evidence to suggest that 70 years is the correct number is just not that abundant, nor compelling. In addition, the number 70 can represent a completed act of God in the earthly realm 7 in divine order 10, 7 x 10 = 70. But when God completes an act, it has no sin in it, unlike the *qualitative* characteristic of a Biblical generation. Therefore, the number 70 qualitatively should not be associated with a Biblical generation.

Some have added the number 70 to 1948, the birth year of the modern nation of Israel, to suggest Christ will return before 2018, 70 + 1948 = 2018. The passage of time has already shown this hypothesis to be incorrect, since the event known as the abomination of desolation would have already occurred by the first half of 2015.

In conclusion, it is unlikely that 70 *quantitatively* represents a Biblical generation. Seventy years more closely represents a completed act of God in the earthly realm in divine order; one *not* associated with sin. Sin is *qualitatively* inherent within a Biblical generation. Therefore, defining a Biblical generation as 70 years is far less likely to be correct compared to 52 years, which represents God's priestly group 13 coming around full circle 4: 13 x 4 = 52.

CHAPTER 31

THE TRANSITION PATTERN OF 6 TO 7 (6/7)

The number 6 is the number *given to man by God* and/or *to the imperfect efforts of man*. It is a number that *falls short* of God's perfection in the earth realm. This perfection is symbolized by the number 7.

God appears to use 6 to 7 as numerical pattern to mark a *transition* between the imperfect works and efforts of man 6 and the completion of a perfect act of God in the earth realm 7. It also appears to mark *a spiritual transition from man to God*.

This pattern is frequently seen in the Bible. The implications of this Biblical numerical transition pattern may turn out to be very profound to our modern era, as will be described in the hypothetical model presented later in this book. Here are just a few examples of the *6/7 transition pattern*.

Examples of the 6/7 transition pattern seen in the Biblical text.

God made the Earth in 6 days and rested on the 7th day.

EXODUS 20:11 (NKJV)

For *in* **six days** the LORD made the heavens and the earth, the sea, and all that *is* in them, and rested the **seventh day**. Therefore the LORD blessed the Sabbath day and hallowed it. [Bold type added]

The 6/7 transition pattern related to mankind's work within a week

EXODUS 31:15 (NKJV)

Work shall be done for **six days**, but the **seventh** is the Sabbath of rest, holy to the LORD. Whoever does any work on the Sabbath day, he shall surely be put to death. [Bold type added]

LEVITICUS 23:3 (NKJV)

Six days shall work be done, but the **seventh day** *is* a Sabbath of solemn rest, a holy convocation. **You shall do no work *on it*;** it *is* the Sabbath of the LORD in all your dwellings. [Bold type added]

EXODUS 16:26(NKJV)
THE GATHERING OF MANNA IN THE DESERT

Six days you shall gather it, but on the **seventh day**, the Sabbath, there will be none. [Bold type added]

A Hebrew servant was to labor for 6 years and be set free on the 7th year.

EXODUS 21:1–2 (NKJV)
THE LAW CONCERNING SERVANTS

Now these *are* the judgments which you shall set before them: If you buy a Hebrew servant, he shall serve **six years**; and in the **seventh** he shall go out free and pay nothing. [Bold type added]

Moses' ascent to the Lord on the mountain represents a man's *transition* towards God. This occurred on the 7th day.

EXODUS 24:16–18

The glory of the LORD dwelt on Mount Sinai, and the cloud covered it **six days**. And on the **seventh day** he called to Moses out of the midst of the cloud. Now the appearance of the glory of the LORD was like a devouring fire on the top of the mountain in the sight of the people of Israel. Moses entered the cloud and went up on the mountain. [Bold type added]

The days of Sivan 6 to 7 in the Hebraic calendar marked historical events that were essential for mankind to transition back to God.

God gave Moses the Torah, God's instructions to mankind for walking out a godly life on Earth. The Jewish people celebrate this event in a holiday called *Shavuot* or *Pentecost*.

The Jewish celebration of Shavuot occurs in the Jewish calendar on *Sivan 6 to 7*. The 6/7 transition of these dates numerically mark the transition from mankind *without* God's instructions for living to mankind *with* His instructions for living. These instructions are essential for *a spiritual transition from mankind to God*.

Some Christians also celebrate Shavuot or Pentecost specifically on the dates *Sivan 6 to 7*, not only to mark Moses' ascent to Mount Sinai to receive God's instructions for living, but also to mark the time, hundreds of years after Moses, that God's Holy Spirit (3) was made available to reside in the spiritual hearts of human beings. The anniversaries of these events do not always fall on a Sunday, as was the belief of the Sadducees, who were wrong on many doctrines, including resurrection. God's numerical consistency strongly suggests that both events occurred on the same Jewish calendar dates: The Sivan 6 to 7-time period. Given the way we see God using multitudes of numbers in a remarkably consistent manner, why wouldn't He do the same regarding these two huge events? Another numerical support for Shavuot occurring on Sivan 6 to 7 comes from the timing of the Jewish Feast of First Fruits and the counting of the omer. I will not be detailing this latter subject in this book, although the evidence is substantive. I may present this information in a post-book blog.

Another related numerical observation is that Sivan is the *3rd month* in the Jewish calendar. As such, Sivan is befitting of the month that God's Holy Spirit (3) was made available to mankind.

The 6/7 transition pattern can also be seen in two widely recognized Jewish symbols.

The Jewish temple menorah contains *6 branches* on the side of a *central 7th candle*. It represents the 6/7 transition pattern.

The Menorah

According to the *Temple Institute* in Jerusalem, "The menorah, made from a single piece of solid gold, stands in the southern side of the Sanctuary. Each morning a priest prepares and rekindles the wicks. The central wick, known as "the western candle" is required to burn perpetually. The oil and wicks of this candle are changed in such a fashion as to insure that it will never be extinguished."[15]

The *Jewish Star of David* also illustrates the "*6/7 transition pattern*". It has 6 points. These 6 points form *6 areas* that surround *a central 7th area*. This pattern emphasizes that the *focus* of man (6) should *center* upon God (7).

The 6/7 pattern seen in the continents of the Earth

God made the world in *6 days* and rested the *7th day*. Isn't it interesting and consistent with God's use of numbers in creation that the Earth contains *7 continents*? Moreover, only 6 out of the 7 continents contain *nations of men*. Antarctica does not. There has never been a permanent human population living in Antarctica. Countries from some of the other 6 continents have made territorial claims within Antarctica, but other countries do not recognize them. In fact, in the *Antarctica Treaty* as of 2015, 53 countries have agreed to set aside disputes over territorial sovereignty indefinitely. So even in this Earth that God created, we see consistency in His use of the pattern of 6/7 in that *6 continents* have been given to nations of mankind, and the *7th continent*, Antarctica, has not.

Prophetic implications of the 6/7 transition pattern

Why has God used the 6/7 transition pattern so frequently in the Bible? And what hidden meanings could this pattern contain? Is God using this pattern to tell us something about a future event?

1. The thousand-year period 6/7 transition that we are now in.

So far in this chapter, I have shown examples from the Bible of the 6/7 transition pattern applied in terms of *days* and of *years*. Is there any Biblical support to apply the 6/7 transition pattern to *thousand-year periods*?

The following Biblical passage was written by the apostle Peter. He is specifically talking about when Yeshua will return to Earth. The day He returns is also known as the Day of the Lord. In this description, Peter refers to the fact *"that with the Lord one day is as a thousand years, and a thousand years as one day."* Remember, God is outside our dimension of time. 1 day = 1,000 years.

2 PETER 3:2–4, 8–9
THE DAY OF THE LORD WILL COME
That you should remember the predictions of the holy prophets and the commandment of the

Lord and Savior through your apostles, knowing this first of all, that scoffers will come in the last days with scoffing, following their own sinful desires. They will say, "Where is the promise of his coming?

But do not overlook this one fact, beloved, ***that with the Lord one day is as a thousand years, and a thousand years as one day***. The Lord is not slow to fulfill his promise as some count slowness, but is patient toward you, not wishing that any should perish, but that all should reach repentance. [Bold type and Italics added]

Remember, God is outside our dimension of time. So the greater significance is the actual *representative use* of numbers, and not their *units of time*. Therefore, we have a Biblical basis to consider thousand-year periods together with the 6/7 transition pattern in relation to when Yeshua will return to Earth; the Day of the Lord. I will refer to this as *the 6th to 7th millennial transition pattern*.

It has been approximately 6,000 years from the time of Adam and Eve. It appears likely that God will give mankind the choice, for approximately 6,000 years, to try to live successfully and peacefully without Him. Mankind will try various forms of human government during this time, but all will eventually fail.

In November 2015, we are currently in the Hebraic year 5776. This is also in the *6th Hebraic millennium*, or thousand-year period. The *7th Hebraic millennium* will begin the first day of the Hebraic year 6,000. This concept is exactly analogous to the fact that in the year 2000 we started living in the 21st century; not the 20th century.

In the current Hebraic year, 5776, we are currently inside the time frame of the *6th to 7th millennial transition period*, but still *224* years before *the start* of the 7th Hebraic millennium. Will Yeshua return *before* we reach the exact start of the 7th Hebraic millennium in the year 6000? Judging by key and essential prerequisite signs in the world today that have already been fulfilled and by others that are in the process of being fulfilled, it appears quite likely that humanity may not make it all the way to the 7th Hebraic millennium. Until humanity makes it to the Hebraic year 6000, the *6th to 7th millennial transition period* remains a valid timeframe to watch for the expected return of the Yeshua, the Messiah.

Is there any Biblical support to the argument that it's possible for Yeshua to return *before* the exact beginning of the 7th Hebraic millennium? After all, God usually completes His perfect act in the earth realm at the numerical marker of 7. Yes, there is a valid Biblical support for an earlier return. Yeshua has told us that He would *have to* come back *early*, because if He didn't, no human being on Earth would be saved!

MATTHEW 24:21–22
For then there will be great tribulation, such as has not been from the beginning of the world until now, no, and never will be. And **if those**

days had not been cut short, no human being would be saved. But for the sake of the elect **those days will be cut short**. [Bold type added]

Therefore, in addition to the established pattern of *6/7* applied in terms of *days* and of *years*, we can also see the probable future manifestation of the "6/7 transition pattern" validly applied in the broad window time frame of *thousand-year periods*. This probable future manifestation is related to the return of Yeshua to the earth realm at the event known as the Day of the Lord.

2. The 6/7 transition pattern in the Israeli Six-Day War

In about 2004 or 2005, I signed up with *The History Channel* to receive emails about their upcoming two-week broadcast schedule. When I received their email, I went through it and picked out the upcoming programs I wanted to watch. In one of their emails, I saw that they were going to broadcast a show on the Israeli Six-Day War. I wanted to remind myself to watch this program, so I printed out the detail of this program and placed the printout on my end table. A few days later, I re-read this program description and noticed that the very day the Israelis captured the Temple Mount was on June 7, 1967.

Seeing this, I jumped with enthusiasm. Many people knew that the Israeli Six-Day War was fought in 1967, but probably few knew and understood the significance of the fact that the very day they captured the Temple Mount in Jerusalem was June 7th! The Temple Mount is where the first and second Jewish temples once stood. *June 7, 1967* was numerically and spiritually an extremely significant day.

Numerically, if you haven't seen it yet, June 7, 1967 is symbolic of a double-number repeating pattern of 6/7 transition, June 7, 1967 = 6/7 / 67. As a *double-number repeating pattern*, it should have some association with Yeshua. I will describe this numerical association in the next two chapters of this book.

Spiritually, June 7, 1967 also represents *the day* of a 6 to 7 transition, during which the nation of Israel reconnected to their spiritual heritage via the Temple Mount, *from man to God*.

June 7, 1967 used in the calculation of the last Biblical generation

Because the Israeli capture of the Temple Mount occurred on a *double 6/7 pattern*, this event should somehow be associated with the Second Coming of Yeshua. More specifically, until proven otherwise, this day of transition (6/7 – 6/7) marks the day that *began the count forward of the last Biblical generation*. This was the day of transition from man to God of the generation that will not pass away before the return of Yeshua to Earth.

So if the numerical evidence suggests that the last Biblical generation started in the year 1967, as Israel made a 6 to 7 spiritual reconnection to God, and if the number of years in a Biblical generation is approximately 52 years, then we can attempt to draw a hypothetical conclusion.

If we add 52 years to 1967 we get the year 2019. But if we consider only whole numbers, we need to use *one-day shy of 53 years* in the calculation. This is because, for illustration, a person is 52 years old up until the very last day before his 53rd birthday. On his 53rd birthday, he is no longer 52. Therefore, if we add 53 years to June 7, 1967 and subtract one day, we get *June 6, 2020*, which, interestingly enough, is also historically known as D-Day, from the invasion of Normandy, France, in World War II. If *all* these numbers and interpretation of Matthew 24 are correct, the *latest* Christ will return will be June 6, 2020. He could return at a time *before* this date.

However, the possibility that Yeshua could return prior to this date will be forever invalidated if we do not see the abomination of desolation occur *in the year 2016*. If we do not see this event in 2016, this speculative hypothesis would be null and void. We would either have to use a new starting date, or a different number to represent a Biblical generation (for example 60 or 66 years), *or consider that the entire speculative process is invalid.* This and other possibilities will be discussed further in the speculative hypothetical model presented in Part III of this book.

3. The Jericho 6/7 pattern: a link to Christ's Return (77)

Do we have ADDITIONAL symbolic numerical evidence to support the argument that the *6 to 7 transition pattern* will be linked to the return of Yeshua? Absolutely! This will be discussed in full detail in the

Part II, Chapter 33, because the appearance of *the 6 to 7 transition pattern* in the Biblical story of Jericho also is intricately linked to the meaning of *two 7s*.

4. The UN's 67th year of operation: a possible major transition into world government

Finally, of brief note here is that fact that the UN's 67th year of operation was October 2012–October 2013. The 6 to 7 transition pattern represented in this year also overlaps the 12 to 13 transition pattern. Both transitional numerical patterns could be marking the beginning of the final 7-year period.

THE 12 TO 13 TRANSITION PATTERN

In ancient Israel, the Levitical tribe of priests was the 13th tribal group to the other tribes that lived on 12 allotments of land. You have also seen this pattern repeated as Yeshua is the 13th to the group of 12 disciples, which represented His initial wise counsel and the start of His divine government on Earth.

The number 12 is God's number for *wise counsel and/or divine government*. The last 7-year period of Daniel in the prophecy of Daniel's 70 Weeks of Years should be a time during which God's wise group of people 12 see an abundance of evidence that points to Yeshua's soon return. A numerical marking of this last 7-year period by the numbers 12 and 13 seem appropriate and consistent with how God has used these numbers. Although it cannot be proven at this time, the possibility exists that the season of time between the Gregorian calendar years

2012–2013 and the UN's 67th year of operations may have marked the beginning of the final 7-year period.

How would the above be possible? The October 2012–October 2013-time frame could have been a much greater transition towards one world governance than is fully recognized today. We already have proof that major agreements concerning world government were made in secret during this time period and only later revealed to the public. In March 2013, negotiators met in secret to develop the framework for the current Iranian nuclear deal. These secret negotiations were made public only after November 2013. Many other non-public deals could have been made during this period. This period may turn out to have been a very under-recognized beginning of the final 7-year period (also foretold in the Bible) preceding the return of Yeshua. As such, it could be numerically marked by the *6/7 transition pattern* seen in the UN's 67th year of operation. The concept that a major non-public agreement between leaders was made in secret is based on Scripture and is a potentially key component to the speculative hypothetical model that will be discussed later in this book.

CHAPTER 32

THE NUMBER TWO (2) – THE KEY TO UNLOCKING THE NUMERICAL TREASURE ROOM

A s I mentioned in the introduction to this book, I began receiving information on Biblical numbers after the 9/11 attacks on America. For several years, I had received insights on numerous numbers and patterns. Streams of numerical revelation continued to come my way as I lived my normal daily life. The numbers were being placed right in my face at times. I was just receptive and I gladly received them. This was not an effort of man. It was a fairly effortless process. I collected the information on scraps of paper and threw them into a big plastic container. I had information on the numbers 1, 3, 4, 6, 7, the pattern of 6 to 7, 8 through 13, the seasons for war in the USA and many others. But all during this time, I never received any insight on how God was using the number *2*.

Then, one night in about 2005, I was watching Perry Stone's television program, *Manna Fest*, on TV. I was only semi-watching the program at first, as I was drifting off to sleep. Then, a man named Dr. Bryan

Cutshall came on the program as Perry Stone's guest. He had written a book called, *Unlocking the Prophecy Code*. Dr. Cutshall started talking about Biblical numbers. I do not remember his exact words, because I was in the process of coming out from my semi-sleep state. But he indicated that Jesus' (Yeshua's) number is the number 2. He's the Second Adam. He will be coming to the Earth two times." I quickly snapped fully awake mode.

I sat up, and out of a little bit of jealousy, the first thing I said to myself was, "Hey! I'm the numbers guy! Why didn't I get that information?!" I thought about this later and realized that one person was not supposed to get all the answers on any topic. Members of God's Church are supposed to work together. This subject is described in *1 Corinthians 12:26*, in which the apostle Paul talks about the Body of Christ. I do not think that God is going to give *any one person* all the answers. One reason, most likely, is that if one person even seemed to have most of the answers, who would most people choose to follow? Probably, that one person!

Well, very soon thereafter, I purchased Dr. Cutshall's book. It contains truly great insights on many subjects hidden in Biblical codes! I highly recommend you read this book. But my biggest personal take away was about the number 2, because the number 2 later became a numerical key that unlocked the door to a treasure room filled with amazing numerical information, which I will show you in the next chapter.

Some of the insights described below were pointed out in Dr. Cutshall's book, *Unlocking the Prophecy Code*.[16] The other insights are my personal observations.

People who study Biblical numbers have said that 2 is the number of Jesus (Yeshua). However, it is *more precise and more meaningful* to say that Yeshua's *base* number is the number 2, for reasons I will also show you in the next chapter.

a. The Bible teaches that Yeshua will come physically to the earth realm *two* different times.[16]

He has already been in the earth realm once. The first time He came as the Lamb of God. The *second* time He will come, He will be a Lion, a King of Kings conquering with great wrath. The *second* time is referred to as the *Second* Coming of Christ.

b. The Second Testament in the Bible is specifically all about Yeshua.

Although there are over 300 specific prophecies in the First Testament that unquestionably point directly to Yeshua, the *Second* Testament is *all* directly about Yeshua. It is commonly said that the First Testament is Christ concealed and the *Second* Testament is the Christ revealed.

Here is a related observation I already described in Part I, Chapter 4: OTHER TERMINOLOGY USED IN THIS BOOK, but it is worth repeating here in this chapter on the number 2.

A related side question: Did you ever wonder why God wrote the Ten Commandments on *two* tablets of stone? After Moses broke the first set of tablets, Moses had to carve out the Ten Commandments on *two* tablets a *second* time? God certainly could have written all Ten Commandments on one stone if He wanted to, either on a bigger stone or with a smaller font! Or He could have written them on 3 or more tablets. Was there a specific reason why God chose *two* stone tablets? Two tablets were a foreshadowing of the fact that eventually there would be *two* Testaments, the First and Second Testaments. The Second Testament again being specifically about Yeshua.

c. **Yeshua is referred to as the *Last* Adam, a term also known as the *Second* Adam. Yeshua is also the *second* manifestation of the Godhead. The *second* Man in the following Scripture is the Lord Yeshua.**[16]

1 CORINTHIANS 15: 44–47
There is a natural body, and there is a spiritual body. And so it is written, "The *first man Adam* became a living being." **The *last* Adam** became a life-giving spirit. However, the spiritual is not first, but the natural, and afterward the spiritual. The first man *was* of the earth, *made* of dust; **the second Man *is* the Lord from heaven**. [Bold type and Italics added]

THE NUMBER TWO (2) – THE KEY TO UNLOCKING THE NUMERICAL TREASURE ROOM

d. God uses multiple *second-choice patterns* in the First Testament to foreshadow Christ as the *Second* Adam.

In each of the following examples, God chose the *second*-born to fulfill His spiritual work and promise on the Earth.[16] All of these *2nd*-born men are in the generational lineage that lead to Yeshua. All of these *2nd*-born men are numerical foreshadowings of Yeshua (2).

1. Cain (the first born of Adam and Eve) and Abel (the *second* born)
2. Aaron (Moses' older brother) and Moses (the *second* born)
3. Ishmael (the first born of Abraham) and Isaac (the *second* born)
4. Esau (the first born of Isaac) and Jacob (the *second* born)

e. Right from the beginning of Yeshua's earthly life, He was associated with the number 2. (Note also that this is found in Matthew chapter *2*.)

MATTHEW 2:16 (NKJV)
Then Herod, when he saw that he was deceived by the wise men, was exceedingly angry; and he sent forth and put to death all the male children who were in Bethlehem and in all its districts, from **two** years old and under, according to the

time which he had determined from the wise men. [Bold type added]

f. Yeshua summarizes and simplifies all *613 commandments* found in the Torah of these commandments into *2* basic commandments.

There are *613 commandments* or instructions in the Torah, the first 5 books of the First Testament. Was one of the reasons Yeshua chose to summarize these 613 commandments down to 2 commandments to tell us again that His base number is the number 2?

> **MATTHEW 22:36–40**
> "Teacher, which *is* the great commandment in the law?" Jesus said to him, " *'You shall love the LORD your God with all your heart, with all your soul, and with all your mind.'* This is *the* first and great commandment. And *the* second *is* like it: *'You shall love your neighbor as yourself.'* **On these two commandments hang all the Law and the Prophets."** [Bold type and Italics added]

I will discuss additional insight concerning the number of Biblical commandments also in the next chapter. This information is really cool and is very consistent with how God uses numbers.

g. Yeshua always has at least 2 witnesses.

Yeshua has 2 witnesses at His resurrection, 2 witnesses at His ascension and 2 witnesses foretelling His return during the last 3.5 years. He also was with 2 when He was transfigured on a high mountain top.

LUKE 24:1–4
HE IS RISEN

Now on the first *day* of the week, very early in the morning, they, and certain *other women* with them, came to the tomb bringing the spices which they had prepared. But they found the stone rolled away from the tomb. Then they went in and did not find the body of the Lord Jesus. And it happened, as they were greatly perplexed about this that, behold, **two** men stood by them in shining garments. [Bold type and Italics added]

ACTS 1:10

And while they were gazing into heaven as he went, behold, **two** men stood by them in white robes, and said, "Men of Galilee, why do you stand looking into heaven? This Jesus, who was taken up from you into heaven, will come in the same way as you saw him go into heaven." [Bold type and Italics added]

REVELATION 11:3
THE TWO WITNESSES

And I will give *power* to *my* **two** witnesses, and they will prophesy one thousand two hundred and sixty days, clothed in sackcloth." [Bold type and Italics added]

MATTHEW 17:1–3
THE TRANSFIGURATION

And after six days Jesus took with him Peter and James, and John his brother, and led them up a high mountain by themselves. And he was transfigured before them, and his face shone like the sun, and his clothes became white as light. And behold, there appeared to them **Moses and Elijah**, talking with him. [Bold type added]

At this transfiguration event, Moses was the witness representative of the Law and Elijah was the witness representative of the prophets.

Why did Yeshua always have *2 witnesses*? Is He establishing this consistent use of the number 2 as a basis to teach us even more about Him through numbers? The answer is "yes," and I will show this to you, again, in the next chapter.

h. **Yeshua sends 70 of His followers out to preach His Word *under the authority of His Name*. He also sends all of them out in groups of *2*.**

This is consistent with *Yeshua's name* being numerically associated with His *base* number 2.

LUKE 10 (NKJV)
THE SEVENTY SENT OUT

After these things the Lord appointed seventy others also, and sent them **two by two** before

His face into every city and place where He Himself was about to go. [Bold type added]

i. **Chapter/verse numerical confirmation of the Biblical text:** *Psalms 2:7*

PSALMS 2:7 (NKJV)
I WILL DECLARE THE DECREE:
The LORD has said to Me,
'You *are* **My Son**,
Today I have **begotten** You. [Bold type added]

In this verse, we can see that the *chapter number* is the same as Yeshua's base number 2. The Biblical *text* is referring to Yeshua. And we see that the *verse number* 7 is consistent with a completed act of God in the earth realm, as Yeshua was begotten and born in the earth realm.

Here is another example of how a person reading the Bible can gain an additional level of understanding by knowing that Yeshua's base number is the number 2.

I was asked to lead a Bible study in 2014. Instead of looking just at the *future prophetic* applications of God's numbers, I wanted to share something a bit different with the study group. I didn't know exactly what I was going to talk on. So, I just started randomly scanning the Bible, and within about two minutes, I came upon the following passage.

ACTS 7:9–13

And the patriarchs, jealous of Joseph, sold him into Egypt; but God was with him and rescued him out of all his afflictions and gave him favor and wisdom before Pharaoh, king of Egypt, who made him ruler over Egypt and over all his household. Now there came a famine throughout all Egypt and Canaan, and great affliction, and our fathers could find no food. But when Jacob heard that there was grain in Egypt, he sent out our fathers on their first visit. And on the second visit Joseph made himself known to his brothers

I was amazed at the numerical parallel that I saw in these verses. So, I decided to use these Scriptures as part of my Bible study lesson.

At the Bible study, I asked someone to read the Scripture out loud. Then I asked the group, "Does anyone see any implications of the numbers seen in the text of these verses?" I believed that most people hadn't even focused in on the numbers. So I asked the same person to reread the passage a second time, but in that time I asked him to specifically pay attention to the numbers. So he did. I will highlight the numerical representations in ***bold italics***.

But when Jacob heard that there was grain in Egypt, he sent out our fathers on their ***first visit***. And on the ***second visit*** Joseph made himself known to his brothers . . .

I then said to the group, "Do you see the parallel foreshadowing Yeshua? Any time you see something related to a number 2, stop to consider if you can see a connection to Yeshua, because His base number is 2. In this case, Joseph did not reveal himself to his brothers on the *first visit*, just like Yeshua is hidden in the First Testament. But on the *second visit*, Joseph revealed himself to his brothers, just as in the *Second* Testament, Yeshua is revealed to all His spiritual children."

The study group was enlightened by this additional depth of understanding that came out of paying attention to the numbers in the Scripture. Likewise, when you read Scripture, pay attention to the numbers: You may uncover additional meaning contained within the Biblical text.

One Prophetic Implication of the Number 2 for Today:

The combination of two Scriptures suggests that Christ's Second Coming may occur around *2,000 years* after His First Coming.

Yeshua, as the Good Samaritan, pays the innkeeper two days' wages and promises to return.[16]

LUKE 10:33–35
But a Samaritan, as he journeyed, came to where he was, and when he saw him, he had compassion. He went to him and bound up his wounds, pouring on oil and wine. Then he set him on his own animal and brought him

to an inn and took care of him. And the next day he took out **two** denarii[a] and gave them to the innkeeper, saying, 'Take care of him, and whatever more you spend, I will repay you **when I come back**.' [Bold type added] [a] Luke 10:35 A *denarius* was a day's wage for a laborer.

Combine the prior passage with the following passage. The following passage was also discussed in the previous chapter on the *6/7 transition pattern*.

2 PETER 3:8–9 (NKJV)

But, beloved, do not forget this one thing, that with the Lord **one day** *is* as **a thousand years**, and **a thousand years** as **one day**. The Lord is not slack concerning *His* promise, as some count slackness, but is longsuffering toward us, not willing that any should perish but that all should come to repentance. [Bold type added]

This yields the interpretation: *2 days x 1,000 years = 2,000 years*. So not only will Yeshua come to the earth realm on 2 separate occasions, as consistent with His base number 2, but also this mathematical interpretation suggests that the time between Christ's first and second comings to the earth realm will be approximately 2,000 years.

There are other major prophetic implications involving the relationship between the number 2 and Yeshua's return. These will be discussed in the next chapter.

CHAPTER 33

TWO SEVENS (TWO 7S) – HOW THE LORD APPEARS TO BE USING TWO SEVENS

I consider the probable meaning of *two 7s* to be the most fascinating symbolic information in this book. This information has the potential to make a contribution to prophetic understanding that is, on one hand, *timeless*. On the other hand, only the passage of time will determine if there are valid links between this information and *the timing* of a 7-year window for the return of Yeshua.

Here is the conceptual basis for the meaning of two 7s. If 7 represents a completed act of God in the earth realm, and 2 is Yeshua's base number, then when God completes an act in the earth realm *specifically related to Yeshua*, this event will be represented by *two 7s*.

Yeshua's *ultimate* act of perfect completion in the earth realm *will be His return to the Earth*. The major goal of this chapter is to provide you with an overwhelming amount of evidence that supports the assertion that God is using **two 7s** *to numerically symbolize and foreshadow His return at the last battle* *of Armageddon. Two 7s* also numerically represent the Word of God. You will see that two 7s can take the forms of 77, 49 (7 x 7), 14 (7 + 7), or these numbers multiplied by a power of 10, such as 490 or (70 x 7). All forms point to completed acts of God in the earth realm *specifically related to Yeshua.*

The following is my story about two 7s. As I mentioned in the PREFACE of this book, please pay specific attention to *how the information was obtained.*

The story begins back in 2004. I had just learned about the existence of the seasons for war in the USA. I had corresponded by email with Jack Van Impe Ministries about Dr. Van Impe's calculations on the number of years that made up a Biblical generation. *I presented an excerpt of this email correspondence in* CHAPTER 30, THE NUMBER FIFTY-TWO (52) – A Biblical GENERATION? The main reason that I initiated this email correspondence was to find out the specific details of Dr. Van Impe's calculations. I also wanted to share with Dr. Van Impe that the number of years he had calculated to be a Biblical generation (approximately 52 years) lined up with the number that was occurring in the seasons for war in the USA.

A total of 3 emails were exchanged in the correspondence. The first was simply a request for Dr. Van Impe's calculations. Excerpts of the other two are reproduced below. Please pay particular attention to the **bold** font text.

From: "…." <…@jvim.com>
To: <..MMagee..@...>
Sent: Wednesday, **October 06, 2004** 3:05 PM
Subject: FW: generation-calculation

Hello Michael,
Here is the information that you requested. We do not make transcripts available but I wanted to send this to you.

According to Matthew 1:17, there were 42 generations between Abraham and Jesus Christ. This covers a period of 2,160 years. Divide the 2,160 by 42 and it comes to **51.5** years for a generation.

Matthew 24:32-35 tells us that the generation that sees Jerusalem captured by the Jewish people will also witness the Return of our Lord.

Israel is the fig tree, and when Israel captured Jerusalem in 1967, we believe this started the countdown. You add 51.5 to 1967, and it comes out to 2,018.

This is why, though we are not setting a specific date, we believe that the Lord's Return could happen between now and 2018.

God Bless you,
XXXX
Media Manager

Excerpt of my email reply:

From: <..MMagee..@...>
To: "...." <...@jvim.com>
Sent: Wednesday, **October 06, 2004** 9:23 PM
Subject: Re: generation-calculation

Thank you for your response. I would like to share what I believe the Lord has shown me. These are 3 timelines for "seasons for war" in the USA. . . . . A friend has taken this information and placed it **on a word document which I have attached** . . .

. . . Dr. Van Impe's work below is mutually complementary to these 52 year seasons for war, in that it shows God's repetitive use of 52 in his creation. Others include the fact that if we ... give 7 days to a week, this . . . results in 52 weeks in a year. **Also there is a mathematical relationship between 52 and 40, another number God uses frequently in the Bible. This is 40 divided by 52 equals 0.77.**

[I do not yet know if there is any specific significance to 7 v. 77 v. 777. The thought that there may be comes from a parallel between 6, the number of man and 666. Perhaps this will be additional information God will reveal in the future.]

. . . I hope this will be a blessed sharing of God's information. I am sure that you will use it according to His guidance and wisdom.

Michael Magee, MD

I had no further email correspondence to Dr. Jack Van Impe Ministries on this subject. About a year after this email correspondence, I saw the Perry Stone television program with Bryan Cutshall that I talked about in the previous chapter. Dr. Cutshall had made a case that the number 2 was Yeshua's number. Another day or so went by. As part of my normal routine, I occasionally review and delete *old emails*. In doing so, I came across the email exchange I had with Dr. Jack Van Impe Ministries a year earlier and I re-read the emails.

The first thing that came to my mind was that the ministry's media director probably thought I was nuts for including a statement that was fully off the main topic of the war seasons. He didn't know me from Adam. In the email, I included a tangent of thought that pondered why when you divided 40 by 52 you get 0.77 (rounded to 2 decimal points) and not *0.7* or *0.777*! I even put brackets around the thought tangent. The media director probably thought, "Who cares whether the answer is *one* 7, *two* 7s or *three* 7s?! It's just math!" But when I was writing this email, this question really *bothered me in my spirit*, for some unknown reason, I suspected that this could have a deeper meaning; something more than just a mathematical curiosity. So I included in this tangent, "Perhaps this will be additional information God will reveal in the future."

The second thing that came to my mind as I re-read the email, however, was a potential connection to what I had heard Dr. Bryan Cutshall say a few days earlier. He had said that Jesus' number is the number 2. And in my old email, the answer to the mathematical equation contained *two* 7s! So the next question that came to my mind was, "*Are the two 7s contained in this mathematical answer somehow related to Yeshua?*"

I then got an unusual push in my spirit to re-examine the equation. Please verify the following on your own calculators if they go out to 26 decimal points. If you do not round up to two digits:

$$40 / 52 = 0.769230769 \ldots$$

I normally would have done nothing more with this equation, but *another* unusual push in my spirit prompted me to want to know what number should *replace* 52 as the equation denominator to yield an answer that contained *7 decimal places*, and that is precisely:

$$0.7700000$$

Now, if I had been mathematically astute, I simply would have rearranged the equation this way to get my answer.

$$40 / 0.7700000 = ??$$

But if I had done it that way, I probably would have not perceived the fascinating information that was contained in the answer. The way I worked the equation was by the trial and error method. First try, I did this:

$$40 / 51.9 = 0.7707129 \ldots$$

So this was little closer result. Now normally for my second attempt, I would add just *one more* digit after the 0.9 decimal place. But for my second attempt, the thought came to mind to jump ahead and add *two more* digits. I will tell you why I chose to add *these specific two digits*, **48**, in a little bit. Here was my second attempt:

$$40 / 51.9\underline{48} = 0.77000077000077 \ldots$$

After this result, the unusual push in my spirit was accompanied by a totally unexpected, soft voice heard in my mind. I can assure you that I am not a guy who hears voices in his mind. This was definitely not normal. But it did happen on this occasion.

The best way to describe this voice is to say that it was a voice of low volume and slightly deeper in tone than the way my normal thinking voice sounds. To help you understand this statement, consider that *your* normal mind's voice probably does not sound like a high-pitched voice, like that of a famous cartoon character mouse. If you really think about it, your own mind's voice probably has its own tone.

The unexpected voice of a different tone said softly and simply, *"Go further."* So I added 4 more digits, 0514, to the denominator of the equation. I reached my intended goal on the *third* try. Was this a spiritual completion that took 3 times? Maybe.

$$40 / 51.948\underline{0514} = 0.7700000$$

Although I was excited about achieving the goal in 3 attempts, I was even more excited by the broader significance of the number in the equation denominator on the *second attempt*, 51.948. I refer to this equation as the *77 Mathematical Equation*.

$$40 / 51.948 = 0.77000077 \ldots$$

If you haven't perceived the significance of this yet, the *77 Mathematical Equation* contains the number that God uses to represent *a time of trial or testing that leads to a new cyclic beginning* or *birth*, 40 (please also refer back to the chapter on the number "40"), and divides this number by the *birth month* and *birth year* (in the Gregorian calendar) of the modern nation of Israel, May 1948! May 1948 is represented by 51.948 (5 / 1948). Stated another way, there is a mathematical association between 40, Israel's birth month and year, 5 1948, and 0.77000077. If Yeshua uses two 7s to represent His completed act on Earth, then the timing of His return could be mathematically related to the birth month and year of the modern nation of Israel.

This is a mathematical confirmation of something that Bible prophecy scholars have believed for years based solely upon the Biblical text: the literal rebirth of the nation of Israel (40 and 51.948) had to become a reality in order to validate *the proper timing* of other prophecies related to the return of Yeshua (77). One of the most common rebuttals about the return of Yeshua is that people have been talking about His return for almost 2,000 years and have always been wrong. This is true, but the key prerequisite that had to be in place did not occur until 05/1948. If the rebirth of Israel had occurred in *any other month* or in *any other year*, the *77 Mathematical Equation* would not exist to validate the timing of Yeshua's return.

As a reminder, the *77 Mathematical Equation* is also one of the five points I made in Part II, Chapter 30 supporting the assertion that a Biblical generation is quantitatively defined by approximately 52 years.

At this time, I will also mention that Jewish scholars have also noted something special about the year 1948. Remember, in Part I, Chapter 12, I said that there was evidence that God is still using *both* the Hebraic and Gregorian calendars. The following is one of those examples. Jewish scholars have noted that Abraham, the father of the Hebraic nation, was born in the *Hebraic* calendar year of *1948* and that the modern nation of Israel was born in the *Gregorian* calendar of year *1948*.

I later modified the *77 Mathematical Equation* to reflect the worldwide impact that the birth of the modern nation of Israel has had on the Earth. To reflect this *worldwide impact*, I used the number 4, because this number describes something that *starts* in one place on the Earth and then eventually *spreads* or *expands full circle* around the Earth or to the *four corners* of the earth. I repeated 51.948 three additional times in the denominator of the equation for a total of 4 times. So this is the result. Please confirm this with your own calculator. Make sure that subsequent repetitions have a 0 in front of the 51948, like this: "051948".

$$40 / 51.948051948051948051948 = 0.770000000000000000000000077$$

Notice that in this answer the *two* 77s act as numerical bookends that surround a total of 22 zeros. Additional significance of this equation can be appreciated by looking at the following Biblical Scriptures, in which Yeshua describes Himself as both *the First* and *the Last*.

ISAIAH 44:6 (NKJV)
I *am* the **First** and I *am* the **Last**; Besides Me *there is* no God. [Bold type added]

ISAIAH 46:9–10
for I am God, and there is no other;
I am God, and there is none like me,
declaring the end from the beginning
and from ancient times things not yet done,
saying, 'My counsel shall stand, and I will accomplish all my purpose,' [Bold type added]

Note that *the end* of the answer to the mathematical equation is two 7s, 77, which is also seen being *declared at the beginning* of the answer.

REVELATION 1:8 (NKJV)
"I am the Alpha and the Omega, *the* **Beginning** and *the* **End**," says the Lord, "who is and who was and who is to come, the Almighty. [Bold type added]

REVELATION 1:11 (NKJV)
saying, "I am the Alpha and the Omega, the **First** and the **Last**," [Bold type added]

REVELATION 21:6 (NKJV)
He said to me: "It is done. I am the Alpha and the Omega, the **Beginning** and the **End**. [Bold type added]

REVELATION 22:13 (NKJV)
"I am the Alpha and the Omega, *the* **Beginning** and *the* **End**, the **First** and the **Last**." [Bold type added]

Wow! So the appearance of 77 acting like numerical bookends to 22 zeros is in line with and is numerically symbolic of the fact that Yeshua is *the First* and *the Last*.

It is also interesting that there are 22 zeros, not only because 22 is comprised of Yeshua's base number twice (two 2s), but also because numerically there are also 22 letters in the Hebraic alphabet. Yeshua is numerically present on both sides of the entire Hebraic alphabet. The words of His Torah were written originally with this alphabet. And *Yeshua is this Word made flesh.*

JOHN 1:1–5, 9–14
THE WORD BECAME FLESH

In the beginning was the Word, and the Word was with God, and the Word was God. He was in the beginning with God. All things were made through him, and without him was not any thing made that was made. In him was life, and the life was the light of men. The light shines in the darkness, and the darkness has not overcome it.

The true light, which gives light to everyone, was coming into the world. He was in the world, and the world was made through him, yet the world did not know him. He came to his own, and his own people did not receive him. But to all who did receive him, who believed in his name, he gave the right to become children of God, who were born, not of blood, nor of the will of the flesh, nor of the will of man, but of God.

And ***the Word became flesh and dwelt among us***, and we have seen his glory, glory as of the only Son from the Father, full of grace and truth." [Bold type and Italics added]

To recap the series of unlikely events that led to uncovering the meaning of two 7s, I had emailed Jack Van Impe Ministries. Words in that email included an unusual statement that questioned why an equation had two 7s in its answer. Also included in this email was the statement, "Perhaps this will be additional information God will reveal in the future." About a year after this email was written, that was exactly what happened. The hidden additional information was revealed. Dr. Bryan Cutshall's information on the number 2 acted as *a key* to unlock the code that revealed the *77 Mathematical Equation.* I was amazed at the way all of this information came together and at its profound significance.

But this was just the start of the amazing numerical journey. There was much more discovery ahead on the path to uncover and confirm the meaning of two 7s.

The Word of God is Numerically Symbolized by Two 7s

After I found out about the *77 Mathematical Equation,* I just continued my normal daily life. But on occasion, I would share the equation with all who seemed to be interested.

In the Dallas area, in what I believe was the 2005-2006 time frame, one of the churches started to interpret the individual numbers contained within a given Hebraic year. So they were interpreting the corresponding Hebraic year of 5766 at that time. I thought the process was quite interesting, but I wanted to look at years that were in the future; ones that would line up with the beginning of the next season for war. By this time, my numerical radar screen had been receiving recurrent hits on the year 2019. I will illustrate the numerical convergence on 2019 in Part III of this book. The year 2019 happens to correspond to the Hebraic year 5779. When I saw 5779, I duly noted the **77** contained in the Hebraic year. Because I was so fascinated by the information pertaining to the *77 Mathematical Equation*, I wanted to interpret the numbers contained within the Hebraic year 5779. So I asked my Orthodox Jewish doctor friend and looked for other sources on Hebraic numbers. But through my own efforts, I could not find any information that helped. Back in 2006, the informational content on the internet was not nearly as vast as it is today.

So, I temporarily gave up on my efforts to find information that would help me interpret 5779. Then one day, early in the morning at work, one of the nurses who had heard me talk about Biblical numbers, walked into the building. *Out of the blue*, she handed me her copy of *Restore!* magazine. This magazine is published by Dr. John Garr, the founder and president of Hebraic Christian Global Community. The magazine is dedicated to restoring the Biblical Hebraic heritage to the Christian believer. The nurse, who gave me the magazine is of Jewish heritage and believes that Yeshua was and is the Messiah. She said to me, "Dr. Magee, I brought you this magazine, because I thought it may be something that you would be interested in. But I am sorry because I just spilled my coffee all over it!" I looked at the magazine and it was drenched in coffee and the pages were sticking together. I thanked her for her thoughtfulness.

As I peeled apart the wet pages, I immediately saw the information I had unsuccessfully sought for weeks! Was this another orchestration by God or just another coincidence in a very long string of coincidences? Perhaps I was not supposed to have found the information on my own efforts. In my opinion, the Lord prompted a fellow believer, *who had no idea* that I was in the process of looking for Hebraic number symbolism, to give me the exact information that I had been looking for. Also, as a side note, I had no idea that 7 years later, I would meet and be taught by Dr. John Garr in the small church I now attend.

This is what I saw when I peeled open the wet pages of the magazine.

The Hebrew Alphabet

BY KARL D. COKE, PH. D.

The Hebrew alphabet is a series of "word pictures." Each letter is a drawing of an ancient item within the culture of these Semetic people. According to the Gesenius *Hebrew-Chaldee Lexicon,* the following is a list of the Hebrew letters with their word picture and numeric value: When one views the Hebrew alphabet through its original word pictures, it appears as parables. Each letter contains

Revelation 4:1. H a door was opene heard was as it w said, 'Come up h must be hereafte

Perhaps the g phabet by Jesus said of himself, ' and the end, the

The apostolic came to us in Gr transliterated for is the first letter (last. So, we hav (*Alpha* and *Ome* said in Hebrew.. ing the alphabet *HaDesha* (New "I [am] the a (*Al*

1	ALEPH	א	1	Ox head	
2	BETH	ב	2	House	
3	GIMEL	ג	3	Camel	
4	DALETH	ד	4	Door	
5	HE	ה	5	Window	
6	VAU	ו	6	Nail, or hook	
7	ZAYIN	ז	7	Weapon	
8	CHETH	ח	8	Wall	
9	TETH	ט	9	Snake, or serpent	
10	YODH	י	10	Hand	
11	CAPH	כ	20	Hand, or bird in flight	
12	LAMED	ל	30	Ox goad	
13	MEM	מ	40	Ocean wave	
14	NUN	נ	50	Multitude, or fish	
15	SAMECH	ס	60	Prop, or to support	
16	AYIN	ע	70	Eye	
17	PE	פ	80	Mouth	
18	TZADE	צ	90	Signet	
19	QOPH	ק	100	Ax head	
20	RESH	ר	200	Head	
21	SHIN	ש	300	Teeth	
22	TAU	ת	400	The end	

Gre

HE

Each Hebraic letter has an associated *numerical value* and an associated *word picture*. Note the *word picture symbolism* for 5, 7, and for 9, **5** is symbolized by a window, **7** a weapon, and **9** a snake or serpent. I found out later from other sources that the specific weapon that 7 represented was a *sword*. Once I learned this, I remembered that the Bible talked about the Word of God as being like a double or two-edged sword.

HEBREWS 4:12

For the *word of God* is living and active, sharper than any *two-edged sword*, piercing to the division of soul and of spirit, of joints and of marrow, and discerning the thoughts and intentions of the heart. [Bold type and Italics added]

In this Scripture, the text presents the conceptual analogy between God's Word and a double edged-sword. So I wondered, "If a 7 represents a sword in Hebraic word picture symbolism, could *two 7s* represent a *two-edged* sword? If true, then could *the Word of God* be numerically symbolized by *two 7s*?

In order to answer these questions, I searched the Bible for other examples of a two-edged sword in relation to Yeshua.

REVELATION 1:16–17

In his right hand he held seven stars, ***from his mouth came a sharp two-edged sword***, and his face was like the sun shining in full strength.

When I saw him, I fell at his feet as though dead. But he laid his right hand on me, saying, "Fear not, *I am the first and the last*, and the living one. I died, and behold I am alive forevermore, [Bold type and Italics added]

REVELATION 2:12

And to the angel of the church in Pergamum write: "**The words of him** who has *the sharp two-edged sword*." [Bold type and Italics added]

And here is the passage in which we see the Word of God symbolized pictorially as a *sharp two-edged sword*, used to destroy the armies of the Antichrist that will be surrounding the city of Jerusalem at the last battles of Armageddon. Please also note the chapter number 19 and relate it to how God often uses the number 19. (Please refer back to Part II, Chapter 28: THE NUMBER NINETEEN.)

REVELATION 19:11–16; 19–21

Then I saw heaven opened, and behold, a white horse! The one sitting on it is called Faithful and True, and in righteousness he judges and makes war. His eyes are like a flame of fire, and on his head are many diadems, and he has a name written that no one knows but himself. He is clothed in a robe dipped in blood, and the name by which *he is called is The Word of God*. And the armies of heaven, arrayed in fine linen, white and pure, were following him on white horses. *From his mouth comes a sharp sword* with which to strike down the nations, and he will rule them with a rod of iron. He will tread the winepress of the fury of the wrath of God the Almighty. On his robe and on his thigh he has a name written, *King of kings and Lord of lords.*

And I saw the beast and the kings of the earth with their armies gathered to make war against him who was sitting on the horse and against his army. And the beast was captured, and with it the false prophet who in its presence had done the signs by which he deceived those who had received the mark of the beast and those who worshiped its image. These two were thrown alive into the lake of fire that burns with sulfur. *And the rest were slain by the sword that came from the mouth of him* who was sitting on the horse. [Bold type and Italics added]

From this passage, we can see that *the Word of God* is being *pictorially* symbolized by a sharp *two-edged sword* to slay the army of the beast (the Antichrist). This battle will occur at the time of Yeshua's return to Earth. If a sharp two-edged sword can be *numerically* symbolized by *two 7s,* as suggested by the Hebraic word picture alphabet, then we have support from the Biblical text that *two 7s* can also be associated with Yeshua's return to Earth. This interpretation of the Biblical text is also consistent with the numerical concept that if *7* represents a completed act of God in the Earth realm in general, and *2* is Yeshua's base number, then when God completes an act in the earth realm *specifically related to Yeshua*, this event will be represented by two 7s.

The crucifixion of Yeshua at Golgotha, the place of the skull, was a completed act of God specifically related to Yeshua. This event was not only marked by two 7s in the date, Nisan 14 (7 + 7), but also by the symbolism of two 7s hidden within the cross. If you turn a sharp *two-edged sword* (two 7s) upside down and stick it into the top of a skull, you have the image of the cross upon the top of Golgotha. This is an image of the Word of God (two 7s) conquering death: a completed act by Yeshua in the earth realm (two 7s).

In the attack of 9/11 on America, two 7s are seen both numerically and symbolically foreshadowing Yeshua's return to the Earth. Before I present that information, I want to share with you much more evidence *from the Biblical text* that God is using two 7s to foreshadow His return to the earth realm.

Does the Biblical Story of the Battle of Jericho Foreshadow Yeshua's Return (Two 7s)?

Is it possible that Yeshua's return to the earth realm was foreshadowed numerically over 3,400 years ago at the Battle of Jericho? At first, you may think that this is a pretty absurd question. So much time will have elapsed between the two separate events. But remember, God is outside of our time dimension and He uses numbers consistently throughout the ages. The following observations support the assertion that God gave *specific instructions* to the Israelites at the Battle of Jericho that were not only meant for them, but also meant *for your benefit today.*

The Battle of Jericho was the first battle of the ancient Israelites in their conquest of the land promised to them by God. Biblical historians and some archeologists have dated the Biblical story of Jericho to around *1400 BC.*[17.] (Interestingly enough to me from the numerical perspective, this number is a representation of (7 + 7) X 100= 1,400.) The Israelites had just completed their extended 40-year penalty period in the desert. Consistent with the meaning of a 40-year number, that time of trial and testing was over, and they were embarking on the new beginning of entering their Promised Land.

God provided the victory to the Israelites at Jericho *in a very unusual way.* And it appears likely that God did it this way for specific reasons. The city of Jericho was surrounded by very formidable defensive walls. The defensive walls consisted of two separate walls built upon a rising embankment. Some have estimated that the two walls viewed by the Israelites from the bottom of the embankment would have appeared to be 10 stories high.[18] For an illustration of this wall, please visit http://www.israel-a-history-of.com/walls-of-jericho. html. The following depicts the very unusual way that God gave the Israelites the victory at Jericho. Please read the following passage from the book of Joshua, while paying close attention to *the numbers* and other bold italic type in the Biblical text.

JOSHUA 6:2–5 (NKJV)
THE DESTRUCTION OF JERICHO

And the LORD said to Joshua: "See! I have given Jericho into your hand, its king, *and* the mighty men of valor. You shall march around the city, all *you* men of war; you shall **go all around the city once**. This you shall do **six days**. And **seven priests** shall bear **seven trumpets** of rams' horns before the ark. But the **seventh day** you shall march around the city **seven times**, and the priests shall blow the trumpets. It shall come to pass, when they make **a long blast** with the ram's horn, *and* when you hear the sound of the trumpet, that all the people shall shout *with a great shout*; then the wall of the city will fall down flat. [Bold type and Italics added]

JOSHUA 6:8–11 (NKJV)

So it was, when Joshua had spoken to the people, that the **seven priests** bearing the **seven trumpets** of rams' horns before the LORD advanced and blew the trumpets, and the ark of the covenant of the LORD followed them. The armed men went before the priests who blew the trumpets, and the rear guard came after the ark, while *the priests* continued blowing the trumpets. Now Joshua had commanded the people, saying, *"You shall not shout or make any noise with your voice, nor shall a word proceed out of your mouth, until the day I say to you, 'Shout!'*

Then you shall shout." So he had the ark of the LORD circle the city, going around *it* once. Then they came into the camp and lodged in the camp. [Bold type and Italics added]

Why did God command the Israelite army to march around Jericho one time for **6 straight days** and on the **7th day** march around it **7 times**? With these numbers, you can see that *both* the *6 to 7 transition pattern* and *two 7s* are utilized within this Biblical text. I believe that it is possible that God commanded the Israelite army to march around Jericho in this numerical pattern *more to benefit us today* by giving us a symbolic numerical of foreshadowing of Yeshua's return than to benefit the ancient Israelite army that actually did the marching. The members of Joshua's army probably were not clued into the meaning of the numbers. They were probably most concerned with *obeying God's instructions to the letter*. They knew very well about the 40-year penalty their nation had endured due to the disobedience of the prior generation, and they were highly motivated to avoid a similar fate.

To make this point seem more real to you, let's go back in our minds to the time of the Battle of Jericho to consider a fictitious, but plausible, conversation between two members of Joshua's army.

Let's say that the two soldiers are named Josiah and Samuel. Both are in their early 20s. The army has marched around Jericho one time for the past 5 consecutive days. They are now back in their base camp. It is the dawn of the 6th day.

Josiah: "What are we doing today, the same?"

Samuel: "Yeah. Marching around Jericho once and coming back to camp."

Josiah: "I just don't get it. What's the purpose? The first day we marched, the Canaanites were fired up for battle; ready and watching us from the tops of their walls. On the second day, they watched us with fearful distrust. They thought that we were up to something they didn't know about. On the 3rd day, they watched us with bewilderment. But for the last two days, they just jeered and mocked us. They called us a bunch of pansies and idiots. They even mocked God! And we couldn't even say anything back, because God told Joshua that we couldn't even say one word! I think that they think we're a bunch of fools and losers!"

Samuel: "Just hold on! First of all, it doesn't matter if we understand things fully or not. Foremost, we need to obey God and trust Him. Remember, how our grandfathers made the mistake of not being obedient and of not trusting God. Our nation got the 40-year penalty of staying in the desert. My father's father was in that disobedient army. He just died 2 months ago. He was one of the last members of that army. Now they're all dead."

Josiah: "Yeah, I know. And I'm definitely going to be obedient! I don't want to go down that desert road for another 40 years! But still, it would just be nice to understand."

Samuel: "Well, Joshua said God will give us the victory, if we're obedient. I don't know exactly how that's going to happen. We're supposed to remain silent until after we complete the *7th circle* around the city on the *7th day*. The only noise allowed from us is the *7* rams' horns that the *7* priests are blowing continuously. But when we finish the *7th* circle, the priests are going to give *one long blast* from the trumpets. That's our cue to break our silence and shout. But Joshua still hasn't told us exactly how we're gonna get over those walls. We haven't even built any ladders or platforms! It's gonna be very interesting to see what happens after we shout."

Josiah: "That's for sure! And what's the point of going around Jericho one time for 6 straight days and on the 7th day going around it 7 times? And why did God tell us to have 7 priests blowing 7 trumpets? Just curious. You know, I'm kind of a numbers guy. Nobody else, but us, seems to be curious about the numbers."

Samuel: "That's true. I originally just thought that the numbers are consistent with the fact that

we work *6 days* and hold a Sabbath rest on the
7th day. I get that. The 6 and 7 thing is symbolic
of what we do. But marching around Jericho 7
times on the 7th day doesn't seem like *much rest
to me*! But, I also love looking into the future.
And this may sound crazy. But maybe there is
another purpose for the numbers that is not
specifically for us. Maybe, it's to say something
to people who will live thousands of years in the
future! You know, our historians are writing all
this stuff down. What we are doing could be
important for others, too. We are participating
in an act of God, and God is eternal. We would
be narrow-minded, if we thought that God is
having us do this *7-day march* around Jericho
only for our benefit. There has to be something
more to this!"

The Israelites did march around Jericho in obedience.
For *6 days*, the number given to man, and nothing
happened to the formidable walls around Jericho. But
on the *7th day*, God provided His completed act of
perfection in the earth realm. *It was God* who provided
the victory. Immediately after *the long trumpet blast*,
the people shouted and the power of God flattened the
walls. This is the representation of the *6 to 7 transition
pattern* seen in the Battle of Jericho.

What about the *two 7s* found in the Battle of
Jericho? How do they symbolize Yeshua's return at
the Battle of Armageddon? Let's look at the parallels

found between the two Biblically described battles. At the Battle of Jericho, the Israelite army marched around Jericho *7 times* on the *7th day* (two 7s), with *7 priests* blowing *7 trumpets* (two 7s). Then, after a long blast of the trumpet and shout by the people, God brought down *the walls of Jericho*, which had separated the Israelites from God's gift of victory. When Yeshua returns at the Battle of Armageddon, He will provide victory as He destroys the army of the Antichrist with the two 7s of His *sharp two-edged sword*. In doing so, He will bring down *the wall that currently separates* man from God, in that *all* will literally see Yeshua. There will be no more speculation as to what the Truth is. Two 7s mark the victorious end of *both* battles as God brings down walls of separation. In this way, God uses two 7s in the past Battle of Jericho to numerically symbolize Yeshua's return at the future Battle of Armageddon.

Two other hidden revelations foreshadowing the return of Yeshua may also be seen in the Battle of Jericho. The first of these involves the position of the 7 priests blowing 7 trumpets with respect to the Ark of the Covenant. These priests marched *ahead* of the Ark of the Covenant. The Ark represented God's promise to the people. So the prophetic implication is this: *Two 7s must come first* before God's ultimate promise to humanity will be fulfilled; His return. Later in this chapter, you will see this numerical concept that *two 7s must come first just before Yeshua's return* is also reconfirmed within other Biblical Scriptures.

The second possible hidden revelation seen in the battle of Jericho is that the priests gave *one long blast* from the trumpets before the shout and before *God* brought down the wall. This one long blast is also consistent with the theory that Yeshua will most likely return at the time of the Jewish Fall Feasts. Today in modern Judaism, one long blast of the shofar is given *only* at the very end of Yom Kippur. Will *the wall of separation between man and God* then fall shortly thereafter? Will Yeshua return at this time of the year? The story of Jericho would seem to support this argument.

Even more support for the argument that the Battle of Jericho foreshadows the return of Yeshua.

The story of the Good Samaritan was mentioned previously in Part II, Chapter 32 of this book. Dr. Bryan Cutshall has made the observation that Yeshua is the Good Samaritan in the parable.[16.] This parable not only supports the argument that Yeshua's base number is the number 2, but also the argument that Yeshua will return in about *2,000 years* from the last time He was in our earth realm.

But there's *another* link between the Battle of Jericho and the return of Yeshua that is *hidden* within the Good Samaritan parable. The parable of the Good Samaritan starts out this way:

LUKE 10:30, 33 (NKJV)
Then Jesus (Yeshua) answered and said: "A certain *man* went down *from Jerusalem to Jericho*,

and fell among thieves, who stripped him of his clothing, wounded *him,* and departed, leaving *him* half dead. But a certain Samaritan, ***as he journeyed***, came where he was. And when he saw him, he had compassion. [Bold type and Italics added]

In the parable of the Good Samaritan, *why* did Yeshua include that information that the Good Samaritan's intended journey was to be *from Jerusalem down to Jericho?* Why didn't Yeshua choose two *other* cities, or why didn't He just say, in a generic way, a man was traveling on a road in the country? After all, it was a symbolic parable. Any country road could have worked in a parable. And why did the intended journey *start* in Jerusalem and why was it supposed *to end* down in Jericho? In light of the other information on Jericho I just shared with you, it looks likely that Yeshua *intentionally* chose a road *from Jerusalem down to Jericho*, because this road is the symbolic path He is on. He was crucified in Jerusalem and, *in the end*, He will return at the Battle of Armageddon in a manner like that seen at the Battle of Jericho; that is, at His return, Yeshua will bring down the wall of separation between God and man.

In addition, both battles are numerically marked with two 7s, as I previously explained. Therefore, the Good Samaritan parable not only supports the arguments that Yeshua's base number is the number 2 and that Yeshua will return in about *2,000 years*, as described by Dr. Bryan Cutshall, but the parable also supports the argument that Yeshua has pointed to *Jericho* as part of *the symbolic end* of His intended journey. Jericho is used in both the parable of the Good Samaritan and in the story of the Battle of Jericho for the purpose of foreshadowing Yeshua's return at the future Battle of Armageddon.

Other numerical formats of two 7s in the Biblical text also foreshadow Yeshua's return.

The Bible points to Yeshua's return to the earth realm in many different ways. His return will be the most important event in all of human history. This is why there appears to be so much evidence supporting the argument that He is using two 7s to numerically symbolize His return at Armageddon. These different ways include the use of two 7s in other numerical formats. At the beginning of this chapter, I also mentioned that two 7s can take the formats of **77**, **49** (7 x 7), **14** (7 + 7) or these numbers multiplied by a power of 10, such as **490** or (70 x 7). All formats point to completed acts of God in the earth realm *specifically related to Yeshua*. And all formats also foreshadow Yeshua's return at the Battle of Armageddon.

- **49 (7 x 7 FORMAT) IS SEEN BOTH IN THE *YEAR* COUNT TO THE JUBILEE YEAR AND IN THE *DAY* COUNT FROM PASSOVER TO PENTECOST (OF PESACH TO SHAVUOT):**

The Jubilee Year and (7 x 7) used in terms of years.

God commanded the ancient Israelites to hold a Jubilee celebration every 50 years. They were to count off (7 x 7) weeks of years, or 49 years. After the 49 (7 x 7) years were completed, then the nation would have its Jubilee celebration in the 50th year. This celebration was also a Sabbath rest in honor of God that lasted for an entire 50th year.

LEVITICUS 25:8–12
THE YEAR OF JUBILEE

Count off **seven Sabbaths** of years—*seven times seven years*—so that the seven Sabbaths of years amount to a period of *forty-nine years*. Then have the **trumpet** sounded everywhere on the tenth day of the seventh month; **on the Day of Atonement** sound the trumpet throughout your land. Consecrate **the fiftieth year** and *proclaim liberty throughout the land* to all its inhabitants. It shall be a jubilee for you; each one of you is to return to his family property and each to his own clan. **The fiftieth year shall be a jubilee for you;** do not sow and do not reap what grows of itself or harvest the untended vines. **For it is a jubilee and is to be holy for you;** [Bold type and Italics added]

Pentecost (or Shavuot) and (7 x 7) used in terms of days.

Similar to God's use of two 7s, in the format of *(7 x 7) preceding 50* in the Jubilee commandment, God also uses (7 x 7) preceding 50 in the count from Passover to Pentecost (or Pesach to Shavuot). Starting from the 2nd day of Passover (2 being Yeshua's base number), (7 x 7) *days were completed* before Moses and the exodus of Israelites were given the Torah, God instructions and commandments for living, on Mount Sinai on the 50th day.

Approximately 1,500 years later, also starting from the 2nd day of Passover, at which time Yeshua was crucified, (7 x 7) *days were completed* before about *3,000* people were given God's Holy Spirit (3) in Jerusalem on the 50th day. The latter occurred on the anniversary of the very same day Moses received and the Israelites were given the Torah.

In both of these events, (7 x 7) *days* had to come first before God was with His people in a *new* way. Likewise, when Yeshua returns to the Earth, He will be with His people in a *new* way. The Bible instructs us that all will see Him and all will acknowledge that He is God.

The 2nd day of Passover is also known as Reishit Katzir.[19] On this day, Messiah is represented as the beginning of the 1st harvest of the year. Please do a simple web search for "Reishit Katzir" and then select the result from www.hewbrew4christians.com for an excellent full explanation of this symbolism. This website's use of numbers to count the days of the Omer is consistent with the numerical perspectives I have shown you in this book. Therefore, there is much numerical evidence to support the accuracy of the numerical information presented on this web page.

Interpretation of Two 7s in the (7 x 7) Format that precedes 50

Whether in the yearly count to the Jubilee year or in the day count to Pentecost, the symbolic numerical interpretation is the same. Two 7s, in the format of (7 x 7), must come first *before* a manifestation of God dwells with us. At these times, there are Jubilees: 50= God is with us *by grace* (5) *in divine order* (10). This is numerically represented by 5 x 10 = 50.

The future prophetic implication of two 7s preceding 50 again points to the return of Yeshua at Armageddon. As numerical marker of the future, **two 7s must come first just *before* or at the time Yeshua returns**. Yeshua's return will be a time of great worldwide Jubilee for all who truly trusted in Him.

I have also talked about Pentecost (Shavuot) as a time in the Hebraic calendar that is marked numerically with the *6/7 transition pattern* in Part II, Chapter 31. Shavuot begins when *Sivan 6* transitions to *Sivan 7*. This is appropriate because Yeshua's return will mark the transition from human government (6) to God's perfect government on Earth (7). As such, both the *6/7 transition pattern* and *two 7s* are seen in the day count to Shavuot. The same numerical reality is also seen in the Battle of Jericho. In each case, these two numerical patterns ultimately point to the return of Yeshua through numerical symbolism. Indeed, there is great numerical consistency throughout the entire Bible.

Gematria of the Hebraic word "zayin," which is the word for 7

It is also numerically interesting to note that the Hebraic word for "7" is *zayin*. The gematria or combined numerical value of this word = 67.[20] Therefore, two zayins, or two 7s, could be represented as **67 / 67**. This is the same numerical representation as is the date that the modern nation of Israel captured the Temple Mount in Jerusalem, 6/7/67. Therefore, we have even more evidence that the *6/7 transition pattern* and *two 7s* are integrally related.

Does Leviticus 25:8–10, The Year of Jubilee, also point to a specific season of time, within some future year, that Yeshua may return?

Please look at Leviticus 25:8–10 this time from the Complete Jewish Bible (CJB) translation below. The CJB translation specifies that the shofar blast is *a blast* or *one blast*.

LEVITICUS 25:8-10 (CJB)

You are to count seven *Shabbat*s of years, seven times seven years, that is, forty-nine years. Then, on the tenth day of the seventh month, on *Yom-Kippur*, you are to sound *a blast* on the *shofar*; you are to sound the *shofar* all through your land; and you are to consecrate the fiftieth year, proclaiming freedom throughout the land to all its inhabitants. It will be a *yovel* [Jubilee] for you; [Bold type and Italics added]

Note that the time of year that Jubilee starts is after the shofar (trumpet) blast on Yom Kippur, the Day of Atonement. I also pointed out that *one single long blast of the shofar* was used just before victory at the Battle of Jericho. The symbolism shows up here again. *One single long shofar blast marks both the time of Jubilee and the time when the wall of separation between man and God is brought down.* At the start of the Jubilee year, liberty was proclaimed throughout the land. When Yeshua returns, liberty from war and injustice will also be proclaimed throughout the world.

The use of one single long shofar blast at Jericho, at Jubilee and at Yom Kippur today supports the argument that Yeshua will return just after Yom Kippur in some future year. According to my friend, Rabbi E., the only time of the year that *one single long shofar blast* is used today in Judaism is to mark the end of Yom Kippur. Therefore, this numerical and symbolic evidence supports the many other arguments that give support for a return of Messiah at the time of, or a short delay after, Jewish fall feast after Yom Kippur.

- **490 (70 x 7 FORMAT) IS SEEN BOTH IN DANIEL'S YEAR COUNT TO YESHUA'S RETURN AND IN THE WORDS OF YESHUA REGARDING FORGIVENESS:**

The 70 weeks of Daniel prophecy also numerically foreshadows the return of Yeshua with a format of two 7s that is also 490 years (70 x 7 = 490).

DANIEL 9:24–26 (NKJV)
THE SEVENTY WEEKS

"*Seventy weeks* are determined
For your people and for your holy city,
To finish the transgression,
To make an end of sins,
To make reconciliation for iniquity,
To bring in everlasting righteousness,
To seal up vision and prophecy,
And to anoint the Most Holy.

"Know therefore and understand,
That from the going forth of the command
To restore and build Jerusalem
Until Messiah the Prince,
There shall be **seven weeks** and **sixty-two weeks**;
The street shall be built again, and the wall,
Even in troublesome times.
"And after the **sixty-two weeks**
Messiah shall be cut off, but not for Himself;
[Bold type and Italics added]

In Daniel 9:24–26, the prophet Daniel was told in a vision about the times of *two* earthly appearances of the Messiah. This passage is commonly referred to as the *70 weeks of Daniel*. In this term, one week = 7 years. Therefore, 70 weeks (of years) = 70 x 7 years

= 490 years. As per the Biblical text, 70 x 7 years are decreed to pass before *the Most Holy will be anointed.* The anointment of the Most Holy one will occur when Yeshua returns and is crowned King of Kings, Lord of Lords. This event will occur when Yeshua returns. It is, therefore, appropriate and consistent that this event is again numerically marked by a format of two 7s; in this case 70 x 7 years.

But an additional marker of two 7s has been given to us in this Biblical text. Perhaps God placed this additional numerical marker in the word text to emphasize or re-confirm the meaning of two 7s. The count to 70 weeks of years is not a continuous count. It is broken up in two different ways. First, 70 weeks of years is broken up into 69 + 1 weeks of years, (69 x 7) + (1 x 7) = (70 x 7). Messiah was cut off after a total of *69* weeks of years. I will talk about the last week or final *70th* week of years soon.

The second way the count is broken up involves the 69 weeks of years. Looking more closely at the 69 weeks of years that has already occurred, we can see that 69 is broken up further in an intriguing way. There has to be a deeper meaning hidden here. The breakup of the 69 weeks of years is seen in verse 25, ". . . *That* from the going forth of the command to restore and build Jerusalem Until Messiah the Prince, *There shall be* **seven** *weeks* and **sixty-two** *weeks*" This equals 69 total weeks of years (7 x 7) + (62 x 7) = 69 x 7. Notice *both* the numerical format and *the order* that the numbers appear in the Biblical word text. The inclusion of (7 x 7) is numerically intriguing.

Historically, the rebuilding of the walls and city of Jerusalem took 49 years (7 x 7). But in addition to being a historical reality, is there also *a numerical meaning* why 69 weeks were broken up and ordered in the format of (7 x 7) + (62 x 7)? The numerical reasoning for the breakup is consistent with other uses of (7 x 7). It is to numerically mark the importance of two 7s (7 x 7) in a prophecy that in the longer time frame (70 x 7 weeks of years) points to the time of Yeshua's return. In addition, the numerical format places (7 x 7) in the similar position to what is seen in the *77 Mathematical Equation*, the answer of which is 0.77000077. God is declaring *the end* from *the beginning* in this prophecy of Daniel. The very *beginning* of Daniel's numerical count starts with two 7s (7 x 7). And the end of Daniel's entire numerical count *ends* at (70 x 7). In this sense, we have another manifestation of the answer to the *77 Mathematical Equation*. Therefore, in addition to the more obvious *historical reason* why (7 x 7) was placed *before* the (62 x 7) in the word text of the Daniel's prophecy, there may also be a *numerical reason*. Its placement provides even more numerical support to the assertion that two 7s are used to mark the future return of Yeshua in both formats of (7 x 7) and of (70 x 7).

Therefore, within the prophecy of the *70 weeks of Daniel*, two 7s are used *two different ways*. Perhaps the second time is used for additional emphasis. Both ways add even more support to the assertion that God is using two 7s in various numerical formats to numerically mark His return at Armageddon.

Most Biblical prophecy scholars believe that, in the count to complete the *70 weeks of years*, the clock was stopped when Messiah was cut off after 69 weeks of years. This occurred historically at the time Yeshua was crucified. Therefore, the count to 70 weeks of years is broken up into 69 weeks + 1 week of years. So the question that many who study Bible prophecy are now asking is: "When will the clock restart to finish *the final last week of years?* This final last week of years is also known as the *final 7-year period* or the *70th week of Daniel.* I will present an interpretation concerning what we may or may not see happen in the world at the start of this final 7-year period, in Part III of this book. This interpretation starts from the perspective and strength of how God seems to be using numbers to speak to us. Then the interpretation looks at a Hebraic translation of the Book of Daniel. As such, it differs from the current most popular way of thinking about *the timing* of the final 7-year period.

490 (70 x 7 format) is seen in the words of Yeshua regarding forgiveness. This is also another foreshadowing of Yeshua's return.

Peter asked Yeshua how many times he had to forgive someone. Yeshua's answer was **(70 x 7)** times. Here again, we see a representation of two 7s. Is this somehow numerically related to Yeshua's return at Armageddon?

MATTHEW 18:21–22 (CJB)

Then Kefa [Peter] came up and said to him, "Rabbi, how often can my brother sin against me and I have to forgive him? As many as *seven times*?" "No, *not seven times*," answered Yeshua, "but *seventy times seven*! [Bold type and Italics added]

Most people reading this verse conclude that we are to forgive someone an endless number of times; and that (70 x 7) just represents some big figurative number and not the literal number *490*. Most people conclude that we should not even count the number of times that we should forgive someone. This may be true for our personal application, *but is there also another meaning behind Yeshua's choice of words?* After all, if He meant that we should forgive someone an *endless* number of times, then why didn't He say just that and leave out all the numbers? Did Yeshua choose these numbers to be consistent with the deeper numerical meaning that we have already seen God use for (70 x 7); that is did He choose to use these numbers again to point to His return at Armageddon?

The Bible clearly teaches us that when Yeshua returns to earth, the door to salvation will be shut. After that, there will no longer be forgiveness by God for those who are still alive on this earth and have rejected Yeshua as both Lord and Savior. As I have illustrated in this chapter, Yeshua's returns to earth marked numerically by two 7s in different numerical formats, including (70 x 7). This appears to be the deeper numerical reason why Yeshua told Peter that forgiveness should be

(70 x 7) times. After the (70 x 7), the time limit for humanity expires.

A set time limit is given to humanity, as a whole, for God's forgiveness of sin. It is not infinite. Will this time expire within the next 10 years? Part III of this book will look at the probability of this becoming reality. On a personal level, however, the time limit is different. It expires the moment you die.

- **YESHUA'S PROVISION FOR SIN ON THE CROSS OCCURRED ON THE 14TH DAY OF NISAN (7 + 7 FORMAT).**

God commanded the Israelites to sacrifice a lamb for the Passover. This sacrifice occurs on the day of preparation, on Nisan 14 in the Jewish calendar, before the start of Passover on Nisan 15. Yeshua was the Lamb of God. Accordingly, He was crucified on the same day, Nisan 14 (7 + 7 = 14).

There are 30 days in the month of Nisan. Why did God command a Passover lamb be sacrificed on the 14th knowing ahead of time that Yeshua would also be sacrificed on this very same day? Was this just another random coincidence? Of course not. Again, God appears to be using two 7s to represent a completed act on earth *specifically by Yeshua*. Yeshua's provision for sin was just that; a completed act on earth also numerically marked by two 7s in the date of Nisan 14 (7 + 7). His purpose for coming to the earth realm as the Lamb of

God *was finished*, and He even said so in His last words before He died on the cross.

JOHN 19:30
When Jesus had received the sour wine, he said, *"It is finished,"* and he bowed his head and gave up his spirit. [Bold type and Italics added]

There are 77 generations from Adam to Yeshua
These are listed in Luke 3:23–38.

The number of commandments in the Torah points to Yeshua.

About 4 or 5 years ago, I attended a class taught by an orthodox Jewish Rabbi. I refer to him in this book as *Rabbi E.* In this class, he stated that there were a total of *613* commandments in the Torah, the first 5 books of the First Testament. Immediately, I found that number interesting, because its digits could be divided into meaningful components of *6*, the number given to mankind, and *13*, the number given to the priests or priestly nation. I thought, how cool and appropriate is that? Then Rabbi E. noted that without the temple in Jerusalem, we can only follow *277* of the *613* commandments. Knowing what I know about how God uses the numbers 2 and two 7s, I was even more amazed! 277 can be broken up into the components 2, Yeshua's base number, and 77, the numerical marker for a completed act of God specifically related to Yeshua.

Yeshua chose to summarize *613* commandments found in the Torah down to *2* basic commandments.

However, if one doesn't summarize the 613 commandments, only 277 commandments can be followed without a sacrificial Jewish temple. The last time a sacrificial Jewish temple stood on the Temple Mount in Jerusalem was in 70 AD.

I was amazed by the remaining number of 277 commandments for two reasons. First of all, Yeshua's sacrifice was the ultimate and final sacrifice for sin; *it was finished*. God never left the Jewish people without a means to deal with sin. And the fact that only *277* commandments were left available without a temple is *numerically symbolic that Yeshua's final provision for sin is all anyone needs*. Second of all, if any other number, like 273 or 265 or 312 et cetera, was the true number of commandments that could be followed without a sacrificial Temple, such a connection to Yeshua would be very hard to make, if not impossible, except perhaps the numbers 77 or 140, or 490. Therefore, the remaining 277 available commandments is not a random coincidence. It is another confirmation of how God uses numbers in a consistent way to speak to us today.

Prophetic evidence of two 7s seen in our world today: *The 9/11 attack on America* and *the London 77 bombings.*

The major goal of this chapter is to provide you with an overwhelming amount of evidence that supports the assertion that God is using *two 7s to numerically symbolize and foreshadow His return at the last battle of*

Armageddon. Thus far, I have shown you evidence of this by examining the Biblical text. But now I would like to show you evidence that God has used *two 7s* to speak to us in the world around us today. The following two anecdotes will show you that this *has happened* in two recent major world events.

Two 7s seen in the 9/11 attack on America foreshadows Yeshua's return at Armageddon.

The 9/11 attack on America numerically foreshadowed a warning of judgment 9 upon an unwise group of people 11. This following information will strengthen this assertion even further, and it will also point out that the 9/11 attack on America also foreshadows Yeshua's return at Armageddon through powerful numerical imagery involving *two 7s.*

In October of 2006, for some reason that I do not recall, I started reading a web page on the 9/11 attack on America. The article reviewed the four planes and where each of them crashed. Included in this information were the plane flight numbers. The first plane to crash into the World Trade center was American Airlines flight number *11.* Another plane crashed into the Pentagon. This was the third plane to crash, and it was American Airlines flight number *77.*

Had the flight number of the plane that crashed into the Pentagon been any number but 77, it probably would have continued to be totally meaningless to me. But because I knew, by 2006, the significance of the two 7s, this fact and its symbolic significance hit home like a mighty sledgehammer inside my head!

Here is the significance. Remember earlier in this chapter, I showed you that in Revelation 19 Yeshua will be coming down from the heavenly realm to destroy the armies of the anti-Christ with a sharp *two-edged sword* coming out of His mouth. This two edged sword can be *numerically* symbolized by *two 7s*.

If we could choose only one building in the entire world that most symbolizes *the military might of mankind*, it would have to be *the Pentagon building*. So visualize the following imagery carefully in your mind and appreciate the foreshadowing symbolic analogy: Flight 77 (two 7s) crashing *downward* from the sky above into the *military* building known as the Pentagon foreshadows Christ's return at Armageddon as He descends *downward* from above using His *two-edged sword* (two 7s) to destroy the *military* of the Antichrist.

Please do not misunderstand me. I am *not* suggesting that God caused the planes to crash on 9/11. But rather, I believe that God, *in essence*, has said with this symbolism something like this: "I did not cause your (the terrorist's) evil. But if you are going to perpetrate evil, I am going to put My numerical initials on what is happening. I will turn this evil into My good. For in this tragedy, this wakeup call, I will communicate to My people, to those who will listen, that I will be returning soon! All creation will cry out speaking of My return. For those who want to look at numbers, I will give you numbers!"

And there is another symbolic number to consider in the attack on the Pentagon. The Pentagon is a fairly unique architectural building complex. As its name implies, it has *5 sides*. It also contains 5 pentagonal rings of buildings within the complex. The number 5 is the number for *God's grace*. Consider how this is also perfectly consistent with Yeshua's return at Armageddon. When Yeshua returns at Armageddon, the period of God's grace for salvation 5 is closed.

When I understood that God most probably marked the 9/11 attack on the Pentagon with numbers to foreshadow His return at Armageddon, I was truly in awe.

But if that wasn't enough to convince me that God was using numbers in our world today to speak to us, additional confirmatory information was placed before me as I continued my daily activities. One day, probably in late 2006, I was again watching *The History Channel*. A show came on that detailed the construction of Washington, DC. In this show, they pointed out that Washington, was constructed on the western *77th* meridian of the globe. This caught my eye! I said to myself, "Wait a minute! What is the exact longitude of the Pentagon?" So I looked it up. Where Flight *77* hit the Pentagon, *the longitude is* -**77.058**. Sometime later, I learned that *the height* of the Pentagon is *77* feet. Please do a web search to confirm this for yourself. I also learned later that construction on the Pentagon began **9/11**/1941.

To recap, American Airlines Flight *77* crashes into the Pentagon, a *5*-sided building that symbolizes the most powerful military of humankind; its longitude is at -*77* and it is *77* feet tall. Is all of this just a numerical fluke? How bizarre is it that the height of a major unique building = the longitude it is on = the flight number of a plane that crashes into to it, during the most horrific terrorist attack America has ever faced? Normally, the height of a building, its longitude, and the flight number of the plane that crashes into it should not match. Oh, and by the way, the model of the American Airlines Flight 77 was a **757**; also containing *two 7s* and a 5! And all these numbers, together with the symbolic imagery of the attack on 9/11, foreshadow Yeshua's return at Armageddon.

I cannot gauge the significance of the following, but I present this as a numerical curiosity. Others have noted that President George H. W. Bush, who gave his New World Order speech to the nation on **9/11**/1990, exactly **11 years** prior to **9/11**/2001 was age **77** on **9/11**/2001 (b. 1924) and the U.S aircraft carrier that was later named after him is CVN **77**.

Consider all of the above numerical information about *two 7s* and a 5 in the 9/11 attack on the Pentagon together with the other information I have provided previously on the 9/11 attack in Part II, Chapter 27 of this book. Then add to this the specific parallels between historical events found in the Bible and the 9/11 attack, God's warning to America is clearly documented by Rabbi Jonathan Cahn in his book *The Harbinger* and his video *The Isaiah 9:10 Judgment*. All of this information together provides overwhelming evidence, beyond any chance of random coincidence, that God has spoken to His people today through the 9/11 attack on American in ways that are hidden in symbolism. *God is clearly active in orchestrating specific realities in our world today for the purpose of communicating to those who would open their hearts to Him.*

Two 7s and the *77 Mathematical Equation* seen in the London 77 bombings also foreshadowed Yeshua's return at Armageddon.

It has been my observation that if God wants us to know something, He often confirms things at least another time or by another way. I view the following as such a confirmation of His use of numbers in our world today. **Two 7s** and a **5** showed up in the terrorist bombings of London on **7/7/05**. Note that *two 7s* and a *5* show up in the date. These are the same numbers we saw in the 9/11 terrorist attack on the Pentagon. This event in London is now commonly referred to as the *London 77 Bombing.*

One could consider it a mere coincidence that the numbers *in the date* of 7/7/05 match both the numbers in the Pentagon attack and the numerical symbolism for the return of Yeshua at Armageddon. But there is much more numerical confirmatory evidence that it cannot be just a coincidence. The *77 Mathematical Equation* also conspicuously showed up in the *London 77 bombing.* I could hardly believe my eyes when I saw this in a BBC news article. Recall that the *77 Mathematical Equation* relates 77 to 40 to 51.948, the last of which rounded to whole digits = 52. On 7/7/05 in London, 4 bombs were used. The final death count was 52 innocent people. In the *77 Mathematical*

Equation it doesn't matter whether *4* or *40* is used because the answer still contains *two 7s* (77). And it is not possible to kill 51.948 people. As such, 52 is the appropriate number to consider. Because of these numerical considerations, the association of the *77 Mathematical Equation* to the London 77 bombings is a valid one.

Some people may argue that God had nothing to do with the numbers that came out of the London 77 bombings. They could argue that it was the terrorists who chose to bomb on 7/7 and to use 4 bombs. That could be true. But only God has the power to limit the casualties to 52 innocent people. And if this is still not convincing to you, then consider this: The same BBC article reported that the total number injured in the London **77** bombing was *770* people.

Who, but God Almighty, has the power to limit the number of casualties to 770? If the number of people injured was *any other* number like 768 or 657, et cetera., the argument that God also numerically marked the London 77 bombing like He did with the 9/11 attack on the Pentagon would not be as strong.

All of this is beyond randomness. These numerical markings have a purpose to tell you that God is still speaking to us; that He is doing so in *many ways*, but also including through His use of numbers in major human events, such as in these two major terrorist attacks, that He is doing so with a purpose that you might believe that He is real or that your belief may be stronger that He is announcing His soon return.

Conclusion of the chapter on *two 7s*

I began this chapter stating that I consider the probable meaning of Two 7s to be the most fascinating numerically symbolic information in this book. My goal was to provide you with the *overwhelming amount of evidence* that supports the assertion that God is using *two 7s* to *numerically symbolize and foreshadow His return at the last battle of Armageddon.* You have seen that the information was obtained in a very unusual way, that the interpretation of *two 7s* in various numerical formats shows consistency in *both* First and Second Testaments of the Bible, and that these numbers are conspicuously inherent to two recent major world events. All of this evidence points to the conclusion that *two 7s* is related to Yeshua's return at Armageddon.

One major question still remains with respect to *two 7s*. Will God elect to use *two 7s in the Hebraic calendar year* to foretell *the timing* of His return? I will address this possibility in the hypothetical speculative model found in Part III of this book.

CHAPTER 34

DOUBLE NUMBERS (##'S)

I wrote in Part II, Chapter 34 that it is *more precise and more meaningful* to say that Yeshua's *base* number is the number 2, rather than saying just that His number is the number 2. I have shown you examples of double numbers, such as *two 7s* and a double 67 (**67/67**) in the Gregorian date when Israel captured the Temple Mount. Are there other double numbers to be specifically associated with Yeshua, the second manifestation of the Godhead?

I will present one more possible example in this very brief chapter. If the number 6 is the number *given to man by God*, did God give us something with *two 6s*, or *66*, that specifically relates to Yeshua? From Genesis to Revelation, there are 66 books in the Bible; 66 books given to man. The 66th book, Revelation, is all about the return of Yeshua.

These 66 books do not include the books of the Apocrypha. Revelation is not the 66th book of Bibles that include the Apocrypha. The Apocryphal books were written in Greek after the close of the First Testament canon. Many Bible scholars question whether these books should even be considered to be God-inspired.

If they are not *fully* God inspired, they should not be included as a part of the Bible.

Looking solely at how God seems to be using numbers, the numbers would appear to "vote" that there should only be 66 books.

Here's an anecdotal story that may or may not be coincidence, but it is interesting at the least. Revelation is the last book of the Bible and focuses on *the return* of Yeshua. It specifically mentions the place known as Armageddon or Har Megiddo. This is the valley in Northern Israel that spreads northeast from an ancient militarily strategic town/hill known as Megiddo. Most Bible prophecy scholars believe that this is the valley in which the armies of the world will gather for the last battle at the time of Yeshua's return, the Battle of Armageddon.

I was on the tour to Israel in 2004 with Dr. Irvin Baxter. This is the same tour I talked about that started at the UN in New York City when I talked about the number 6. In Israel, I didn't need to preview the daily tour itinerary. I would just get on the tour bus. I also never looked, with one exception, at the road map, because I was never driving. However, toward the end of the tour, we went to Megiddo by bus. Once there, the tour group walked up to its highest point and looked over the valley where Armageddon is supposed to be fought in the future. Dr. Baxter gave his lesson there, much of which was based on the book of Revelation. He finished his lesson and the tour group headed back down the hill to the bus.

For some reason, inspired or coincidence, for the first time on the tour, I decided to look at the road map I had in my pocket to see where we were. My eyes lit up when I saw that *the one and only major highway*, which was adjacent to Megiddo and bordered most all of the southwest border of the entire valley of Megiddo, was *Route 66*. I ran up to Dr. Baxter, who didn't know me well at that time, and said to him excitedly as I pointed to the map, "You see! I've been telling you that the numbers in the Bible are saying something important! Revelation is the 66th book in the Bible. It talks about Armageddon. And someone from the Israeli government has assigned the number *66* to this one highway that borders this valley! I think this is significant!"

Taking into consideration all that I have been made aware of in the past 12 to 13 years regarding how God uses numbers in the Bible and in the world around us today, I am even more convinced now in 2015 than I was back in 2004, that Revelation should be considered the 66th *and* last book of the fully God inspired Bible.

As far as other Biblically related numbers are concerned, if you see pairs or double digit numbers, like *two 7s, 67/67, 66 or even Psalm 22*, in the Bible or in the world around us in events related to Bible prophecy, consider the possibility that in some way these numbers may be pointing to Yeshua.

PART III

NUMERICAL CONTRIBUTIONS TO THE BIBLICAL END-TIME PROPHECY PUZZLE

CHAPTER 35

INTRODUCTION TO PART III

In Part III of this book, I will show you the season for World War III and timelines of Biblically significant numbers that all converge on the years 2019–2020. This information is factual and not speculative. *Interpreting* what these facts will eventually mean to the world *is* a matter of speculation, because it deals with the future. I will talk about a proper perspective for speculation and provide a hypothetical speculative model based upon substantive numerical evidence and several hypothetical premises that will either be confirmed or made invalid as we move forward in time through the next 10 years to 2026.

CHAPTER 36

WHY A PUZZLE?

Biblical end-time prophecy can be viewed as a jigsaw puzzle. There are different categories of puzzle pieces within the Biblical end-time prophecy puzzle. Included in these are geopolitical pieces, pieces related to technological advancements, religious and social trend pieces, astronomical pieces, and *numerical* pieces.

The Biblical prophecy jigsaw puzzle is different from one that you would buy at a store. A jigsaw puzzle that you buy at a store usually comes in a box with all the puzzle pieces inside. The box top also has a picture of the completed puzzle on it. Therefore, you know exactly what the completed picture will look like. This is different from the Biblical end-time prophecy jigsaw puzzle.

In the Biblical end-time prophecy jigsaw puzzle, we do not have the box top to show us exactly how the completed puzzle will look, and we don't even have all the puzzle pieces available to us. God gives us the missing additional pieces of the puzzle *at His timing*, usually through world events that match up with what His Biblical text has described. For example, prior to the birth of the modern nation of Israel, many interpreted Bible prophecy from the perspective that Israel was only a *figurative* concept involved in the end times. That changed in 1948, because we now know that the existence of Israel in end-time prophecy is a *literal reality*. This reality became a hugely important geopolitical puzzle piece that forced most to think differently about the future return of Yeshua.

Today, you may hear many different interpretations concerning how a future event foretold by Bible prophecy may play out in the world. Until we receive the actual associated puzzle piece for any given expected event, any interpretation is, at best, a reasonable and researched speculation. However, just like with a jigsaw puzzle that you buy at a store, the closer you are to completing the puzzle, the easier it is to see how the few remaining pieces will fit in.

At this time, the biggest and most important missing Biblical prophecy puzzle piece is the answer to the question, "*Who will be the one known as the Antichrist?*" Having this puzzle piece will put to rest many different interpretive scenarios that are commonly debated among those who study Bible prophecy. This puzzle piece will be available when we see the Abomination of Desolation in Jerusalem. At that time, we no longer have to speculate about things like whether there will be a rapture of believers *prior* to the last 7 years of Daniel's 70 weeks or not? If there is no rapture prior to the Abomination of Desolation, then the pre-7-year tribulation rapture theory is wrong. All the interpretations about where the Antichrist will come from and how long we have before Yeshua returns will be moot, because we will know the answers. Moreover, if we are still around, we will have bigger concerns to deal with, because we will have entered the time that Yeshua referred to as the greatest tribulation that the world will ever experience.

I have given examples in Part II of this book showing that God tends to de-emphasize *when* something will happen; however, the fact that we have just recently obtained *substantive numerical data* pointing to the timing of His return (which I shared with you in Part II) is a fact that suggests His return may be soon. It looks probable that God will let us know with certainty the timing of His return *only shortly before* that event occurs.

In Part III of this book, I will figuratively throw the *numerical* puzzle pieces onto the jigsaw assembly table. These numerical pieces should help connect *other categories* of Biblical prophecy puzzle pieces together. Hence, the title of Part III: *Numerical contributions to the Biblical end-time prophecy puzzle.*

Detailing the *non-numerical* Biblical prophecy puzzle pieces from categories is not within the main scope of this book. They can be readily found in other sources. However, I will briefly give you a few examples.

Examples of *geopolitical* pieces: The scattering of the ancient Israelites to the four corners of the earth and the re-gathering of the Jewish people in the re-born nation of Israel. The Bible specifically foretold these events over 1,000 to 3,000 years before they happened. See Deuteronomy 28:64, Deuteronomy

30:3–6, Jeremiah 16:14, Ezekiel 36:19, 22, 24, Ezekiel 37:21–22, Isaiah 11, Amos 9:13–15. Other geopolitical signs: the economic trend of globalization and political movement toward world government.

Examples of pieces *related to technological advancements*: Did you know that Bible prophecy scholars consider today's *explosion in knowledge and travel* as a major end-time sign; one that is specific to people who are alive just before the return of Yeshua? Daniel 12 links *the time of the end* to a time of unprecedented technological advancement not experienced by any other people throughout human history.

DANIEL 12:4

But you, Daniel, shut up the words and seal the book, until *the time of the end. **Many shall run to and fro, and knowledge shall increase.**"*
[Bold type and Italics added]

The explosion of knowledge we are witnessing today has been amazing. When I was in high school and college, the process of obtaining information was laborious and drawn out. If I had to research information for a report, I would have to go to the library card catalog, find books, pull them out of the library stacks, open those books, and then determine if those books had any usable information by physically turning pages. If that library didn't have the book I wanted, the library would try to obtain the book from another library. That other library was often over a hundred miles away from where I was located. If the other library had the book, I would usually receive the book in about a week. Once I got the book, I would look through it to determine if it had any useful information. If it didn't, then it was a waste of time and effort.

Today, one can just speak into a smart phone web search app and get a plethora of information in less than one second! A person doesn't even have to remember the precise details of a topic in order to obtain successful web search results. For example, if you can't remember what product was advertised in the famous spicy meatball TV commercial, simply do a web search or speak into your smart phone web search app: *"TV commercial the spicy meatball."* The amount of stored accumulated knowledge readily available today is truly amazing. We are in the Information Age.

The explosion in travel has also been amazing. From the dawn of civilization to the mid-1800s, the fastest anyone could travel was the speed of the horse. As little as 100 years ago, the majority of people never traveled more than several hundred miles from the place they were born. Fifty years ago, the majority of people in the USA never ventured outside of the nation. In the world today, the distance, speed, and volume of travel has exploded exponentially in recent years past. To appreciate the volume of aircraft travel in one day as seen from outer space, do a web search for the YouTube video: *World Airline Traffic (24-Hour Time Lapse).*

The technology required for the Mark of the Beast: The technological evolution to a cashless society is currently in progress. A future political mandate to buy or sell only with a number is just a matter of time. In all of human history, it has never been technologically possible to institute a cashless financial system until now. Most financial transactions today occur electronically in real time.

Examples of *astronomical* pieces: such as the recent blood moon tetrad season, which I will interpret later in this book.

Examples of *religious and social trend* pieces: The great falling away from the truth of Yeshua and His commandments. The apostle Paul states in 2 Thessalonians that a great falling away from the truth and God's instructions, the Torah, has to come before the return of Yeshua. The time of this great falling away from the truth is also known as the great apostasy.

2 THESSALONIANS 2:2–4 (CJB)

But in connection with the coming of our Lord Yeshua the Messiah and our gathering together to meet him, we ask you, brothers, not to be easily shaken in your thinking or anxious because of a spirit or a spoken message or a letter supposedly from us claiming that the Day of the Lord has already come. Don't let anyone deceive you in any way.

For the Day will not come until after the Apostasy has come and the man who separates himself from *Torah* has been revealed, the one destined for doom. [Italics added]

Today this falling away is occurring at a rapid rate. In the United States of America, God has been removed from our schools, courts and our civil laws. The US Supreme Court ruling of June 2015, which mandates the legal acceptance of same-sex marriage in all states, exemplifies the removal of God's instructions from our civil laws.

When people fall away from the truth, where do they fall *to*? They fall into ignorance, apathy, atheism, false religions and cults, and into the deceptive blurred truth of a global religious melting pot known as *interfaithism*. The latter may be seen manifest as the religion expressed by the COEXIST bumper stickers. The COEXIST movement is also referred to by some as the "can't we all just get along" religion. Interfaithism can also be seen manifesting itself through more structured organizations such as the United Religions Initiative and the ecumenical movement of different faiths toward a global religious umbrella centered in Rome. All may seem to have altruist intent, but in reality, they represent deceptions from the truth, unintended or not. As deceptions, they will cause great harm to those deceived people in the end. Many people believe that humans cannot know any significant truth about God or His existence. This belief is in contradiction to the words of Yeshua.

JOHN 8:31–32
THE TRUTH WILL SET YOU FREE
So Jesus said to the Jews who had believed him, "If you abide in my word, you are truly my

disciples, [32] and you will know the truth, and the truth will set you free."

Within the new global melting pot of the interfaithism deception, Yeshua is not politically correct. Why would the world be doing this? This is a sign of the last days foretold in the Bible. On June 26, 2000, hundreds of delegates from 44 countries and 39 religions around the world met in Pittsburgh at the Carnegie Melon University campus to sign the United Religions Initiative Charter (URI). Carl Teichrib, chief editor of www.forcingchange.org, attended that event. He gives his account of the event in an article called *Blending of the Gods*. In this article, Carl Teichrib asks the following about Jesus Christ (Lord Yeshua the Messiah):

> But how does Jesus Christ fit into the URI agenda? Not surprisingly, I never heard the name of Jesus mentioned at the summit. Nor could His name be brought up. After all, it was Jesus Christ who made it clear in John 14:6, "I am the way, the truth, and the life: no man cometh unto the Father, but by me." The exclusivity of Jesus Christ is in direct contradiction to the goals of the URI, its Charter, and interfaithism in general. Not only does Jesus Christ claim to be the only way to God, negating all other "ways," but He commands His followers to "proselytize" - "teach all nations, baptizing them in the name

of the Father, and of the Son, and of the Holy
Ghost . . ." (Matthew 28:19). And in Acts
chapter one, Jesus proclaims that His message
will be preached "unto the uttermost part of the
earth." **Jesus Christ is not politically correct in
the new global order**. . . [Bold type added]

Please see http://www.crossroad.to/articles2/04/
teichrib-blending-gods.htm for the full article.[21]

My friend, Irvin Baxter of Endtime Ministries, also
attended the URI charter-signing event. He recounts
his experience in Part 1 of his podcast, *The Coming
One-World Religion*. [22]

CHAPTER 37

THE SEASONS FOR WAR IN THE UNITED STATES OF AMERICA AND WORLD WAR III

E very war that the United States of America has ever fought has occurred within regular time intervals or seasons. They are NOT random occurrences. Because they are past history, this fact is irrefutable. The time intervals, in years, between the American seasons for war are also Biblically significant numbers. Seasons for war are also mentioned in Scripture. Because of these two irrefutable facts, an association exists between the Bible and the timing of the past American wars, as well as the next season for war. This chapter will explore the strength of that association and will illustrate these seasons for war. We will be entering the season for WWIII in 2016.

I became aware of the existence of war seasons in the United States around 2002–2003, when I read a book on stock markets. In this book, a 50-year cycle in the United States was briefly described, but was never illustrated graphically. Later in 2003, I read a newsletter on the stock market. This newsletter stated that there was an 80-year war cycle in the United States, but it also never illustrated the cycles. So I wondered, "Is there a 50-year war cycle or is there an 80-year war cycle?" I set my mind on finding the precise answer.

I went to the internet to find out when every United States war was fought. What I came up with initially was just a group of time data points. I examined the data group looking for cyclical patterns. I discovered *three separate timelines* of cycles within the data group. Two of the timelines were defined by *52-year intervals*, not 50-year intervals as suggested by the book I read. The remaining third timeline was defined by an *80-year interval*.

I was amazed when I saw that war cycle seasons do exist. Still, I wanted to find out the statistical strength of what I was seeing. I searched around Dallas, TX, for someone better in statistics than I was, but could find nobody. However, on my 2004 trip to Israel, I did find someone. He had a PhD in statistics, and he just *happened* to be with my tour group! He took one look at the war seasons and immediately said, "This is definitely not random." I then asked him, "Well, can you give me some statistics on this? Some people may want to know."

Whether these numbers are correct or not, I'm not sure, because I am not a mathematical statistician. But this is what he told me: The chances of this information being random are less than 2 percent, at a 90 percent confidence level. Based upon these statistics, I often tell people that I know with greater than 98 percent probability, at a 90 percent confidence interval, when *the season* for World War III will be. I immediately follow this statement by saying that this does *not* mean that World War III will *definitely happen* in the upcoming season; I only know the season. Without further ado, here are the seasons for war in the United States of America.

THE SEASONS FOR WAR IN THE UNITED STATES OF AMERICA AND WORLD WAR III

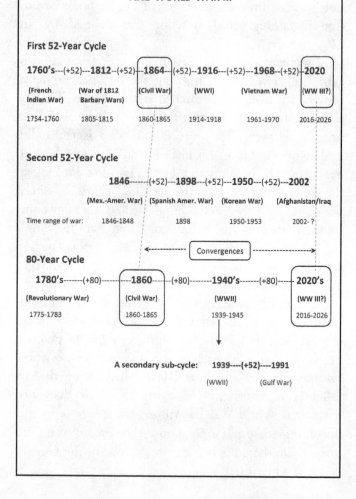

First 52-Year Cycle

1760's---(+52)---**1812**--(+52)---**1864**---(+52)---**1916**---(+52)---**1968**--(+52)-**2020**

(French Indian War)   (War of 1812 Barbary Wars)   (Civil War)   (WWI)   (Vietnam War)   (WW III?)

1754-1760   1805-1815   1860-1865   1914-1918   1961-1970   2016-2026

Second 52-Year Cycle

1846-------(+52)---**1898**---(+52)---**1950**---(+52)---**2002**

(Mex.-Amer. War)   (Spanish Amer. War)   (Korean War)   (Afghanistan/Iraq

Time range of war: 1846-1848   1898   1950-1953   2002- ?

Convergences

80-Year Cycle

1780's-------(+80)----------**1860**------(+80)--------**1940's**-------(+80)------**2020's**

(Revolutionary War)   (Civil War)   (WWII)   (WW III?)

1775-1783   1860-1865   1939-1945   2016-2026

A secondary sub-cycle: **1939**----(+52)----**1991**

(WWII)   (Gulf War)

The following is the interpretation of the war season or war cycle illustration. First of all, know that seasons are windows of time. In time cycle analysis, which is what we are looking at, as long as a time interval length (52 or 80 years) falls within a war's window of time, the cycle is valid. I have placed the *time range* of the war underneath its corresponding war name.

Second, please notice that it takes *3 separate time lines* to account for all wars, except the Gulf War of 1991, which represents a secondary 52-year cycle off shoot from WWII. The explanation for the existence of 3 separate timelines arises out of the following facts: human nature does not change in the natural world; because of this, all generations have their wars; generations are staggered by time. At any one time in human history, multiple generations live *simultaneously* on the Earth, yet their time spans are staggered in relationship to each other. Multiple generations overlap each other. Your generation is living at the same time as your parent's generation, your grandparents' generation, as well as possibly your children's or even grandchildren's generation. As far as wars are concerned, when you are either a child or an elderly person, your generation typically is not the one involved in starting a war. These generations usually have other things than fighting on their minds. This fact contributes to the establishment of 3 separate war time lines. As such, the 3 separate timelines for war are a manifestation of the different generations that are staggered by time. All three are needed to account for all the wars that the United States of America has fought.

Third, note that the 80-year war cycle defines the *major* wars of the United States. 80 is a number similar to 8, a number that God uses to mark a new beginning that will last for eternity. If any of the major wars that define the 80-year timeline had been lost, the political structure of the United States would have been forever changed. Our original founding Constitution would have never been created or would have been replaced by something dictated by the victors of these wars. We would have a different form of government; a different reality of life. For example, unlike World War I (which occurs in a 52-year war cycle time line), if Hitler had obtained the atomic bomb before we did in World War II (which occurs in the 80-year war cycle time line), one could make a strong argument that there would not be a United States today. Our land would be part of the Third Reich. Losing World War II would have been a new beginning that would have *forever changed* the destiny of the United States. A loss of *any* war on the 80-year time line would result in a remnant country that looked little like the country that was founded upon life, liberty, and the God-given unalienable rights of mankind. History has shown that freedom is hard to come by, difficult to keep, and easy to lose.

Fourth, note that the time intervals are numbers that have Biblical significance. In addition to 80, 52 is the number that most likely quantitatively defines a Biblical generation.

Fifth, notice that the Civil War occurs in *two different time lines*. In cycle analysis, this is referred to as a *convergence*. A convergence of cycles occurs when two or more cycles of different lengths hit within the same data window. A convergence increases the probability that a future event will occur. The next convergence will occur in the year 2020, as illustrated. This year is within the middle of the 2016–2026 season for World War III. Because of the cycle convergence, there is a higher probability that World War III will occur within the next war season.

Sixth, every generation has its wars because human nature does not change in the natural world. One thing that does change, however, is *the destructive power of our weapons*. As such, World War III will most likely involve nuclear weapons.

The responsible way to look at the future season for World War III

I always caution people about their interpretation of the upcoming major war season. Just because every war that the United States has fought in the past has occurred in regular, non-random time intervals, it does *not* mean that another war *must* occur in the next season. Using an analogy, I tell people that just because we know when the season for hurricanes in Florida will be, we do not necessarily know with certainty if or when a storm will hit the Florida coastline. When we are in the hurricane season standing on the beach looking out over the ocean, if we start to see ominous storm clouds gathering on the horizon over the ocean, constant high winds with violent gusts, lightning, and 40- to 50-foot ocean waves, then we are seeing *the shorter near-term*

DIVINE NUMERICS AND THE COMING WORLD WAR

signs of a coming violent storm. If we see such signs, we can conclude with high probability that indeed a major storm may be coming to our shores.

A hurricane can hit the coastline at the very beginning or at the very end of the hurricane season or at any time in between. Likewise, a war can also start any time within its season. Based upon all the Biblically related *numerical* information that I have been exposed to, the season for World War III will open up in 2016 and last until 2026. Moreover, based upon both numerical and non-numerical Biblically related information within this 10-year season, the first *very* high risk year for a *nuclear World War III* is 2016, until proven otherwise by the world's safe passage through this year. This speculation is based upon hypothetical, yet substantive, evidence. However, it is still speculative. I will talk about a proper framework for speculation, in the next chapter.

What is the responsible way to look at the upcoming season for World War III? Just as in the hurricane analogy, as we enter the season for World War III in 2016, we need to ask ourselves if we see *the shorter-term signs* of a coming violent storm. On the geopolitical horizon, do we see any dark, ominous storm clouds rolling in? Do we see the huge waves of global unrest crashing into our shoreline? Do we see high winds of political and social discord gusting through the treetops of our nation? Are there ominous signs of lightning and thunder emanating from the financial markets? Assess the probability based upon what you are seeing today, knowing that we are entering the season for World War III. At the same time, keep in mind that just because we will soon be in the season for World War III, it is possible that the storm will never hit. This is the responsible way to gauge the prospect for World War III as we enter the upcoming season for war in 2016.

The Bible talks about seasons for war

Back in 2005, I was working in a hospital procedure room. The radio was playing. The song "Turn! Turn! Turn!" by the Byrds started playing. Someone in the room said, "Those lyrics come from the Bible." I never knew that before this time. Later that day, I went home and looked it up in the Bible. The information comes from Ecclesiastes, Chapter 3. This was written down by King Solomon around 1000 BC, approximately 3,000 years ago!

As God states in Ecclesiastes, Chapter 3, there is a time and a *season* for every purpose under heaven. The Scripture goes on to state that there are times for war (seasons for war). Most people assume that this Scripture is only *figurative*. But by this time of my life, I had knowledge of irrefutable *literal* seasons for war! God shows humanity many *literal* truths in His Word, and this is one of them. I was amazed!

In addition to the *Biblically based* numerical evidence of an upcoming major war season that I have shown, others have identified a similar prospect through *secularly based analysis*. In one such example, 3 different categories of cycles *that all converge on 2016* were identified.

In a 2010 article entitled *Cycles Of War And Peace*, Larry Edelson, the editor of *Real Wealth Report* and *Supercycle Trader*, wrote,

"To summarize ...

→ An important turning point in all economies will arrive **in the middle of 2016,** the peak of the 54-year socio-political cycle.

→ 4.5 and 9-year subcycles, proven out in other economic and financial series, are also lining up as important turning points in a time window ranging **from 2016 to 2017.**

→ The 18-year war cycle is due to hit with maximum force also **in the middle of 2016.**" [bold face type added]

You can find this report in the public domain by web searching: 2010 article entitled *Cycles Of War And Peace*, Larry Edelson.

Historically, nations usually fight wars *after* major socio-political unrest and / or financial collapses. The American and French Revolutions occurred at a time of worldwide economic depression. Similarly, the Great Depression of the 1930s proved fertile ground for the rise of Adolph Hitler. World War II ensued shortly thereafter. Nations do not tend to engage in major wars as long as they are making money. After a major financial collapse, the restraint of prosperity is taken away. Nations get angrier and they are ready to fight. In this sense, the three different cycles that Larry Edelson has identified could *collectively* point to 2016 as a high-risk time for war.

Therefore, the *Biblically based* numerical information suggests 2016 is a very high risk period for the start of a season for World War III *and* Larry Edelson's *secularly based* analysis of three different categories of cycles collectively suggests a similar conclusion. But again, we will have to wait and see. Cycle periods can be non-events.

In conclusion, seasons for war in the United States of America irrefutably exist. A relationship exists between these seasons for war and the Bible. This relationship is shown through the Biblical text and by the Biblical significance of the numbers that define the time intervals between these wars. The next season opens in 2016 and lasts until 2026. It is a season for a *major war* that would threaten the very existence of the United States of America and its Constitution. If a major war occurs in this season, it most likely will be a nuclear war. The upcoming season for war is established by two out of three different war cycle timelines, which come together as a cycle *convergence*. A cyclical convergence represents a period of increased probability that the event will happen. However, this does not mean that war has to occur in the next war season. The responsible way to gauge the prospects for World War III is to consider the analogy between a season for war and a hurricane season. Look at the shorter, near-term future prospects for war. Be alert. Trust in Yeshua and you will be fine whether it happens or not.

CHAPTER 38

THE BIBLICALLY BASED NUMERICAL CONVERGENCE ON YEARS 2019 TO 2020

INTRODUCTION TO THE CONVERGENCE

A s I received and collected the information on Biblical numbers over the past 12 to 13 years, I began to observe that many of the numerical patterns and sequences of *diverse* origin consistently pointed to the years 2019 to 2020. The numbers were not chosen to fit into a 2019 to 2020 scenario. Rather, the numbers figuratively chose this timeframe. But in reality, since numbers inherently cannot choose anything, an important question arises: Could God be using His numbers to point to the 2019 to 2020 timeframe as a clue to future events surrounding Yeshua's return?

The following three Biblically significant numerical data strings initially focused my attention to 2019 to 2020

I have previously described the highly unusual ways items one and two below were received. These items of information have a very low probability of randomness and they are 100 percent consistent with how God uses numbers in the Bible. Something you may never have heard of, *Daf Yomi,* is described in item three. *How* I received this information was also unusual.

1. **Two war cycles converge on 2020, within the middle of the season for World War III.**

2. **The absolute end of a 52-year Biblical generation added to the transitional time of 6/7/67, when Israel recaptured the Temple Mount, equals 6/6/2020. Two numerical double-repeating patterns are illustrated here: 67/67 and 6/6/2020.**

3. **The Living Human Biblical End-time Clock: Daf Yomi.**

One day in 2005, I was working with Dr. G, an Orthodox Jewish gastroenterologist friend of mine. I had recently finished a course of Biblical studies at one of the local churches, so my knowledge about the Bible was much greater than before the course. I started talking about the Torah. Dr. G then mentioned something about the Talmud. I had never heard the word "Talmud" before, so I was a little embarrassed.

But I asked, "What is the Talmud?" Dr. G said that the Torah contained the written instructions, and the Talmud contained oral instructions that were later written down.

When I got home that evening, something prompted me to look up the Talmud on the Internet. I read about it on the website *Judaism 101*. I found it very interesting. Near the end of the article on the Talmud, Daf Yomi was described. *Daf Yomi* means "page of the day." Followers of this daily regimen read one page, and each exactly the same page, of the Talmud every day, worldwide. The article also mentioned that Daf Yomi was started in 1923 by Rabbi Meir Shapiro, and it was at that time in its eleventh cycle. When I saw the word *cycle*, it figuratively jumped off the webpage to my eyes. I did cycle analysis on markets. Because I did cycle analysis, I wanted to know how long each cycle was. Why? I didn't know. Something drove me to find out how long a Daf Yomi cycle in time is. I had no idea whatsoever where this path would end up. So I emailed the author of the article, who lived in Israel and asked him when the twelfth cycle was going to start. Knowing that date would allow me to do a simple division calculation that would yield the cycle length. A few days later, he emailed me back and told me that the twelfth cycle had already started on March 2, 2005. So I did my calculations and found out that each cycle was approximately 7.4 years. I then learned that the thirteenth cycle started on August 3, 2012 and ended on January 5, 2020. I realized I had just come upon yet another convergence on the years 2019 to 2020. How bizarre!

Furthermore, because 13 is the number of God's priests or priestly nations, I thought that it might be connected with the final 7-year period. Remember this concept: *God's priests point the world towards God.* This whole experience was totally unexpected. *All I set out to do initially was to look up the word Talmud,* and I come across *another* Biblically significant timeline that ends in the 2019 to 2020-time frame! Amazing.

If you think about it, Daf Yomi, a practice followed by members of God's priestly nation, 13, actually represents *a living human time clock* that is cycling and counting up towards 2020. If the process of Daf Yomi hadn't started in 1923 and / or if the number of pages in the Talmud were significantly different, the end of the thirteenth cycle would occur at a time that would not have converged with the other information presented in this book.

Later, I discovered that the first cycle of Daf Yomi actually started on the first day of Rosh Hashanah 1923. This was the Gregorian date, September 11, 1923. I made due note of the *9/11* date. This date further strengthens the link between Daf Yomi, a living human Biblical Endtime Clock, and the other information that also portends a future judgment, 9, of an unwise group of people, 11. Please refer back to Part II, Chapter 27, as needed.

To recap the significance of what happened: Out of a simple discussion, the word "Talmud" was mentioned. I went home and looked up the word. In the description of the word, another name, "Daf Yomi," was mentioned. It had a cyclical nature to it and just so happen to include a thirteenth cycle ending on the exact same time frame of the season for World War III and the end of the Biblical generation calculation. To put it even more simply: All I did was look up the word "Talmud," and I was led down a numerical path, totally diverse from previous numerical families of numbers, which also converged on 2019 to 2020! Therefore, just like one and two above, the story about Daf Yomi has a low probability of randomness. And the numerical concepts contained therein are 100 percent consistent with how God uses numbers in the Bible.

In addition to all of the above, note that "2010 to 2019" in the Gregorian calendar corresponds to 5770 to 5779 in the Hebraic calendar. In the Hebraic calendar, all years within this range contain 77. The great significance of two 7s was discussed fully in Part II. For your reference: The Hebraic year 5779 spans from the evening of September 9, 2018 to the evening of September 29, 2019.

Furthermore, one can perform an interpretive analysis on the numbers within 5779 with two different methods: by God's use of the numbers and by Hebraic word pictures. Both interpretations show that 5779 will be related to the return of Yeshua.

Analyzing 5779 based upon *how God uses numbers* in the Bible and in the world around us yields the following. Yeshua will return at Armageddon, 77, at a time when His offer of grace, 5, will be closed and when His judgment, 9, will begin. Corresponding to 5779, the Gregorian year 2019 contains Yeshua's base number, 2, and the number for a final judgment, 19.

An analysis of 5779 with *Hebraic word pictures* yields a similar prognostication. The window, 5, is shut on the serpent. 9, as Yeshua returns to destroy the army of the Antichrist with His double-edged sword, 77.

Very significant numbers involving the US stock market crisis of 2008 and 2009 also suggested a focus upon 5779. As pointed out by Rabbi Jonathan Cahn and many others, the very last closing numerical loss of the Dow Industrial Average, on the very last day of the Jewish year 5768, was 777. Most people have reported this number only to the first decimal point, which was 777.7. However, my friend Randall made an even more fascinating discovery. The precise amount the market fell was 777.*68*. So, the *very last day* of the Jewish year ending in 68 (as in 5768) was numerically marked by point loss ending in .68! Many believe that the 777 was a numerical message from God. But, the additional .68 goes much further to confirm this interpretation.

Because I witnessed the above significant numerical occurrence in the stock market to the hundredth of a point, I was more alert for the next similar occurrence. In the S&P 500 index, the very bottom of the bear market not only contained 666, but was specifically 666.*79*. This suggested to me that, until proven otherwise, the mark of the beast, 666 may be related in some way to the Hebraic year that also ends in 79: 5779.

After my initial attention was directed towards 2019 to 2020, I then looked *backwards* 7 years from 2019-2020 to consider any data consistent with the start of the last 7 years of Daniel's 70th week. This pointed to the years: 2012 to 2013.

Focus on the 2012 to 2013 timeframe

I have already talked about the UN's 67th year of operation, October 2012 to October 2013, as being a potential Biblically prophetic transitional period, with the numerical transitional patterns 6 to 7 and 12 to 13 represented therein. Please see the end of Part II, Chapter 37. In addition to this, we had much speculation building up to "the end of the Mayan Calendar" that occurred on December 21, 2012. Before this date, many people wanted to know my opinion on whether I thought this was the end of the world. I always told them, "First, the Bible teaches that the world will never end. The age of human government is what will end. Second, the end of the Mayan Calendar will likely mark a transition into a new season: the season for the return of Messiah." I based the second statement on the fact that on December 21, 2012, the long count of the Mayan Calendar was *13.0.0.0.0*; again consistent with God's number for His priests or priestly nations, 13.

More Biblical prophetic focus has also been given to the 2012 to 2020 timeframe by the *blood moon tetrad* that occurred on the Jewish Feasts of Passover and Sukkot in 2014-2015. Numerous people believed there was a good chance that something profound was going to happen on those *specific* four dates. However, as these dates approached, I always said, "Although it is possible something significant may occur on those specific dates, it is more likely that the blood moon tetrad marks a *season* of time just like they did in the late 1490s, 1949-1950, and in 1967-1968. It has been my observation that unless God specifically makes an appointed date, such as the tenth day of the seventh month, He usually works in *seasons*." The recent blood moon tetrad may have heralded a season during which there may be major bloodshed at some point in the near future, especially in Israel.

In conclusion, there is an undeniable major convergence of Biblically based numbers on the years 2019-2020. The non-speculative facts concerning this are described above. *How* this convergence will manifest in the future is a matter of interpretative speculation: a type of speculation based upon substantive evidence.

CHAPTER 39

THE SPECTRUM OF SPECULATION – LAYING THE GROUNDWORK FOR PROPER FUTURE EXPECTATIONS

I can't see the future with 100 percent certainty; neither can any human.

Many people think of *speculation* as an activity associated only with gamblers. As such, they want nothing to do with it. But the truth is that *all* people speculate, whether they realize it or not. No human can see the future with 100 percent certainty. Only God, Who is outside the confinements of our four dimensional realm, can see the future with 100 percent certainty. Any time any human makes an assumption about the future, he or she is speculating. The probability of an assumption about the future coming true falls within the spectrum of speculation. The *spectrum of speculation* (SOS) is the broad range of probabilities that exists between two opposite extremes of assumptions associated with an eventual correct reality that will occur in the future.

On one extreme of the SOS, a person can make an extremely reasonable, well-founded speculation about the future that is highly likely to become true. These are often based upon past history and substantive current evidence. If you are a young healthy individual and you were to say, "I'm going to bed tonight and will wake up in the morning"; your assumption about the future is highly probable to be correct. If you say, "I'm going to bed tonight and whether I die in my sleep or not, the sun will still rise in the morning," your assumption about the future has even a higher probability of being correct.

On the other extreme of the SOS, a person can make wild and baseless speculations about the future that are extremely unlikely to come true. For example, if you were to say, "I will be bit by a radioactive fly tomorrow and by next week, I will be able to fly like Superman!" your assumptions are absurdly improbable.

Most speculations of the future by sane, rational people fall closer to the reasonable, well-founded, and more probable end of the SOS.

Interpreting much of Bible prophecy also falls within the SOS, because people are attempting to understand precisely what will happen in the future based upon the facts given to us in the Bible and upon how the prophecies correlate to known current world events.

The hypothetical speculative model, presented later in Chapter 44 of this book, is based upon a large amount of reasonable, researched, Biblically consistent, and well-founded information. Therefore, at least some parts of the model have a reasonable probability of coming true. Understanding where the hypothetical speculative model lays within the SOS will give a proper perspective of future expectations. The unfolding of future events will either confirm or refute the accuracy of the interpretation and hypotheses presented in this model.

CHAPTER 40

LOOKING BACK FROM THE FUTURE

*L*ooking back from the future is a method used to explore more accurate probabilities about the future. This is accomplished by mentally going forward to a future time period, turning around and looking backwards to our present time. This method is similar in many ways to reverse engineering. If you have a completed product or a final goal in mind that you want to make or achieve, but you do not know precisely the steps to take, most often the best chance for success *is to work backwards.*

Because the preponderance of Biblically based numbers and symbolisms presented in this book converge on 2019-2020, we will go in our minds to those years, turn around, and look backwards in time to the present time. If a major event, such as the return of Yeshua, is associated with the 2019-2020 timeframe, then we should see a certain specific confirmation *prior to* Yeshua's return. The specific confirmation could be a rapture of believers in Yeshua, a peace agreement among the Israelis and Palestinian Arabs that confirms Israel's right to exist, or the Abomination of Desolation (AOD).

God may elect to start the final countdown to His return from the perspective of our future looking backwards. Because God is outside time, He can do this with 100 percent certainty. It also makes more sense that God would start from the future at the biggest event in all of human history, His return, and then from that time, count backwards towards our present time the number of days left until His return. Whenever possible, we should attempt to interpret things from God's perspective.

Looking back from the future also best explains the numerical mystery found in Daniel 12: 11–12. The mystery was first introduced to me by Irvin Baxter.

DANIEL 12:11

And from the time that the regular burnt offering is taken away and *the abomination that makes desolate* is set up, there shall be **1,290 days**. Blessed is he who waits and arrives at the **1,335 days**. [Bold font and Italics added]

According to Daniel 12:11, if there will be 1,290 days from the AOD until Yeshua's return, then *who* are those who wait and arrive at 1,335 days, a point in time 45 days *after* Yeshua's return? Will they be a group of people in a jungle or in Antarctica that never got the real-time message that Yeshua has returned, despite the fact that the Bible states that *all eyes* will see Him return? The timing perspective that the event of 1,335 days will occur *after* the event of 1,290 days makes no sense and it contradicts Scripture:

REVELATION 1:7 (CJB)

Look! He is coming with the clouds! Every eye **will see him**, including those who **pierced him**; and **all the tribes of the Land will mourn him**. [Bold font added]

However, the consideration of these same two numbers from the perspective of *looking back from the future* makes a lot of sense. Observe closely how this changes the interpretation. From this perspective, the event of 1,335 days will actually occur 45 days *before* the AOD, the 1,290-day event. Until proven otherwise, the event occurring at 1,335 days prior to the return of Yeshua could be World War III, an event that could kill over 2.4 billion people, one-third of the entire world's population. From the perspective of looking back from the future, if you survive *that event* and continue to survive the entire 1,335 days while remaining faithful to Yeshua, then *blessed are you!* These 1,335 days could also be applicable to those who become believers after an earlier rapture of the church. In any event, the application of looking at things from God's perspective and *looking back from the future* makes so much more sense.

A potential conceptual conflict arises when considering the prospect for WWIII as the 1,335-day event occurring prior to the AOD, the 1,290-day event. This potential conflict is resolved again by attempting to look at things from God's perspective.

In the Gospels, Yeshua says the AOD will occur and *then* there will be great tribulation. I asked one of my Biblical prophecy expert friends, "If one-third of all mankind is killed in WWIII and that occurs prior to the AOD, how can that war not be considered part of the great tribulation?" He told me that the great tribulation will be against those who are believers in Yeshua and have not been killed. Because once believers' earthly bodies are dead, they are with the Lord; no tribulation exists at that time.

If WWIII occurs at the 1,335-day event preceding the AOD, then if you die quickly, there is no tribulation for you. Within the first 45 days after such an event, I would expect that those still alive would be in massive shock. Even those who do not have the Spirit of God living within their hearts may tend to behave in a relatively civil manner. People without God's Spirit have historically always helped in search and rescue missions and have come to the aid of others in need. God's Holy Spirit may still be a restrainer of bad evil behavior on those who are not personally reborn with His Spirit.

However, after 45 days of shock, with food and water running short, and no hope of God within them, these same people could have a behavioral change, especially when the restraint of God's Holy Spirit is removed from those who do not already have God's Spirit within their hearts. This withdrawal of the external restraint of God's Spirit could occur immediately *before* the AOD (see 2 Thessalonians 2: 6–8 below with respect to this timing). Widespread, atrocious violence against others would then begin. Even your once-friendly and trusted neighbors may turn to the dark side. This tribulation would be intensified as God sends a great delusion to those who did not choose to accept Him in a time when there was no panic and tribulation.

2 THESSALONIANS 2:6–8 (CJB)

And now you know what is restraining, so that he may be revealed in his own time. For already this separating from *Torah* is at work secretly, **but it will be secretly only until he who is restraining is out of the way.** Then the one who embodies separation from *Torah* will be revealed, the one whom the Lord Yeshua will slay with the breath of his mouth and destroy by the glory of his coming. [Bold type and Italics added]

2 THESSALONIANS 2:9–12

The coming of the lawless one is by the activity of Satan with all power and false signs and wonders, and with all wicked deception for those who are perishing, because they refused to love the truth and so be saved. Therefore God sends them *a strong delusion*, so that they may believe what is false, in order that all may be condemned who did not believe the truth but had pleasure in unrighteousness. [Bold type and Italics added]

Second Thessalonians 2:9-12 is consistent with **Proverbs 1:22**. If a person waits until *after* the calamity hits, you may not be able to find the One True God.

PROVERBS 1:22, 27–29
How long will scoffers delight in their scoffing
and fools hate knowledge?
Then terror strikes you like a storm and your
calamity comes like a whirlwind, when distress
and anguish come upon you. Then they will call
upon me, ***but I will not answer***, they will seek
me diligently but will not find me. Because they
hated knowledge and did not choose the fear of
the LORD, [Bold type and Italics added]

CHAPTER 41

THE 70TH WEEK OF DANIEL – A HEBRAIC INTERPRETATION

A s a quick reminder, most Bible scholars consider the 70th week of Daniel as the final 7-year countdown to the return of Yeshua. Bible prophecy scholars, however, have various interpretations about *how we will know* when this final 7-year period will begin. Many scholars believe that a rapture of true believers in Yeshua will be the event that marks the start of the final 7 years. Others believe that the signing of a peace agreement that confirms Israel's right to exist will be the event that marks the start of the final 7 years.

Either interpretation could turn out to be correct! Both interpretations are based upon reasonable and sound deductions from Scripture. However, like all interpretative assumptions about the future, both also lay within the spectrum of speculation.

LOOKING BACK FROM 2019-2020

When we were in the year 2007, I went within my mind to 2019–2020 and then looked backwards to 2012–2013. I was a focused observer of world events that would occur specifically from October 1, 2012 to May 25, 2013. Based upon the two prominent interpretations about the event that would mark the start of the final 7 years, I was watching for the sign of a peace agreement in Israel foremost, and a rapture of believers in Yeshua as an alternative, but less probable, event. When neither of the two anticipated events occurred in October 2012 to May 2013, I was forced to re-examine the hypothetical speculative model that I was considering at the time. Re-examination is a method engineers often use: If you attempt to shoot a rocket to space and it doesn't work as expected, you go back to the drawing board in order to uncover what went wrong.

In my re-examination of the hypothetical speculative model, I was led to look at Daniel 9: 27 in different translations. I compared the verse in the New King James translation to the Complete Jewish Bible translation. They imply something *very different* from each other with respect to what we should expect to see regarding the start of the final 7-year period.

DANIEL 9:27 (NKJV)

Then he *shall confirm* a covenant *with many* for one week; But in the middle of the week He shall bring an end to sacrifice and offering [Italics added]

DANIEL 9: 27 (CJB)

He *will make* a strong covenant *with leaders* for one week [of years]. For half of the week he will

put a stop to the sacrifice and the grain offering.
[Italics added]

Most Biblical scholars agree that "he" refers to the Antichrist. In the NKJV, the Antichrist confirms a covenant. If you confirm something, it implies something is already in existence to confirm. Many Bible scholars believe that the covenant the Antichrist will confirm will be God's covenant with Abraham: that descendants of Abraham, Isaac and of Jacob have an eternal right to the land of Israel. This could take the form in a peace agreement that affirms Israel's right to exist in parts of their current land. The NKJV also says the covenant will be confirmed with *many*. What precisely does "many" mean? Ten people or ten million people? This is very non-specific.

On other hand, the CJB translation says something very different. In the CJB, the Antichrist makes *his own* strong covenant, not with "many," but specifically *with leaders*. A big difference exists between agreements made between one nation and another nation and agreements made just among leaders. With agreements made between nations, there are usually official public documents signed, often with video cameras recording the associated events. Agreements just between leaders can be done in secrecy: only revealed sometimes weeks, months or years later.

Although a public peace agreement was not signed in Israel during October 1, 2012 to May 25, 2013, a flurry of significant political activity did start on March

21, 2012. This is the day when President Obama made his first trip to Israel during his presidency. The code name for this trip was Unbreakable Alliance in English, and Brit Amim (*A Covenant of Peoples*) in Hebrew.[23] A barrage of high-level U.S. led cabinet meetings ensued in Israel immediately following President Obama's trip. These meetings continued for several weeks thereafter. During that time what our government told the news media about those talks did not represent the full truth. Yet, nothing was announced about a peace agreement.

After understanding and confirming the CBJ translation of Daniel 9:27 with those fluent in Hebrew from Israel, I began to ask, "How often does the United States of America make significant agreements between only leaders and make these known to the public at a later date? Never? Some of the time? Often? Frequently?"

Several months later in November 2013, the US government announced to the news media that they had agreed on a preliminary framework for an Iranian nuclear deal. I took special note of the news media's reaction. The news media was shocked. They asked how it was possible that the detailed framework the government was announcing at that time happened so quickly. The representative from the US government stated, and I paraphrase, Well, actually we agreed on an initial framework back in March of 2013. We just kept it secret. Wow! Although, this agreement was not one that confirmed the start of the final 7-year period, it did confirm that the US government did make significant agreements during the March to

May 2013 timeframe in secret. Could the agreement that started the final 7-year period also have occurred *in secret* at the time of President Obama's *Covenant of the Peoples* trip to Israel? 2 THESSALONIANS 2:7 in the CJB translation (refer back to page 281) provides Scriptural support, although not proof, that a secret agreement could mark the beginning half of the final 7-year period, as the separation from Torah will be done secretly until the Antichrist is revealed.

Both the NKJV and the CJB translations of Daniel 9:27 will allow some to know with certainty that we will have either a 7-year countdown to Yeshua's return at the Battle of Armageddon (the NKJV translation) or a 1,290-day countdown to His return (the CJB translation).

At this time, I have more confidence in the CBJ Hebraic translation, not only because Daniel was originally written in Hebrew, but also it seems to be more in line with God's past history of letting His people know important events *only shortly before* they happen. For example, God didn't give Moses and the Israelites a 7-day advance notice that He would be saving them by opening up the Red Sea for them to cross. At best, the Israelites received a few moments advanced notice. Likewise, a relatively last-second notice was given to Noah before the Great Flood. I will examine the timing of that in the next chapter.

At this time, we have no certainty about what event will mark the start of the countdown to Yeshua's return. This event could be a rapture occurring 7 years prior to Yeshua's return. Or it could be the signing of a specific peace agreement in Israel. However, until disproven by the passage of time, the interpretation of the CJB translation, in which a secret agreement is made only among leaders, *remains a viable alternative.* In this alternative, we may not know with certainty that an agreement had been made among leaders until we see *the definitive event* known as the Abomination of Desolation. From that event forward in all three interpretations, there will be 1,290 days left.

CHAPTER 42

HOW THE TIMING THAT GOD USED IN THE DAYS OF NOAH MAY BE APPLIED TO US TODAY

One of the descriptions that Yeshua used to foretell of His soon return was a comparison to the days of Noah and of Lot.

LUKE 17:26–29

Just *as it was in the days of Noah*, so will it be in the days of the Son of Man. They were eating and drinking and marrying and being given in marriage, until the day when Noah entered the ark, and the flood came and destroyed them all. Likewise, just as it was in the days of Lot—they were eating and drinking, buying and selling, planting and building, but on *the day* when Lot went out from Sodom, fire and sulfur rained from heaven and destroyed them all. [Bold type and Italics added]

Most people who interpret this Scripture focus on the behavior of individuals on the earth at those times. In the case of Noah, the following describes this.

GENESIS 6:11–13

Now the earth was corrupt in God's sight, and the earth was filled with violence. And God saw the earth, and behold, it was corrupt, for all flesh had corrupted their way on the earth. And God said to Noah, "I have determined to make an end of all flesh, for the earth is filled with violence through them.

But in addition to the behavior of individuals on the earth at the time of Noah, what if God elects to apply the same type of advanced warning that He gave to Noah to His people today? Best estimates are that Noah was given up to 100 years to complete the building of his ark. If we use a 365-day year, that would translate into 36,500 days (36,000 days if using a 360-day year). Except for the very end, all during that time Noah did not know exactly when the flood was going to hit. If Noah asked, he probably was told, "Don't worry about it. Just keep on building the ark." During this time, Noah was probably mocked severely by all, but the other 7 members who were also saved on the ark.

Out of 36,500 days, Noah only received a *7-day advanced notice* that the flood was about to hit! Think about how "last second" that notification was. In terms of the length of a regulation football game, that would be equivalent to the very last 0.07 seconds of the game.

God could elect to translate His timing in the days of Noah to us today. If He does, then before we know with certainty when the final countdown to His return will begin, we should see confirmatory evidence occurring quite unexpectedly and rapidly. The prospect of a rapidly unfolding sequence of events that confirms the timing of Yeshua's return is suggested by His words in REVELATION 22:12 where it reads "And behold, I am coming quickly". (NKJV)

This prospect of a last moment confirmation would negate any thought of a 7-year advance notice by either the signing of a peace agreement in Israel or of a rapture 7 years prior to Yeshua's return. This scenario would also support the CJB interpretation of Daniel 9:27, in which the final 7 years is marked by a secret agreement among leaders alone. God never said in Daniel that the start of the final 7-year period would be public knowledge. He did describe the Antichrist as being involved in the process that would last for 7 years.

When one analyzes the story of Lot from the perspective of timing, a similar conclusion can be made. Lot was given *less than one day's notice* before Sodom was destroyed.

Considering how God *timed His warnings* to Noah and Lot, as well as considering the history of how God most often waits until the last moments before He reveals a major event, like parting the Red Sea in the days of Moses for the Israelites to cross over on dry land, it is less probable today that His people will be given a full 7-year advanced notice of the certainty of His return. The 7-year advance notice possibilities are still viable, however, until they are proven wrong by the passage of time.

In addition to the considerations above, if we were given a 7-year *certain* advanced notice before Armageddon, what do you think most remaining believers on the earth would do? They would probably quit their jobs, sell their homes and move to a mountain fortress. God de-emphasizes *when* events involving His return will happen for a reason. From this perspective, a last moment notification before a disaster revealing the certainty of His return, which could be the events of World War III at 1,335 days and the Abomination of Desolation at 1,290 days before His return, seems more consistent with the known ways of God.

As an interesting aside to how the timing aspect that God used in the days of Noah may be applied to us today, God's numerical signature of two 7's (used to point to His return at the Battle of Armageddon) is also seen symbolically linking the days of Noah to His return. Also interesting is that this information begins in Genesis **7:2.**

GENESIS 7:2-3 (NKJV)
You shall take with you *seven* each of every clean animal, a male and his female; *two* each of animals that are unclean, a male and his female; also *seven* each of birds of the air, male and female, to keep the species alive on the face of all the earth. [Bold type and Italics added]

Here again we see the numerical consistency of 2 and two 7's used in a Biblical event that occurred in the remote past to foreshadow the Lord's future return at the Battle of Armageddon. God is truly of God of order! Everything He does has meaning and purpose!"

CHAPTER 43

HOW THE TIMEFRAME FOR THE LORD'S RETURN MAY BE HASTENED

In Mark 13, Yeshua says that the Abomination of Desolation (AOD) will occur and then there will be great tribulation on the Earth until His return. He says also that if those days were not cut short, no human being would be saved.

> **MARK 13:19–20**
> For in those days there will be such tribulation as has not been from the beginning of the creation that God created until now, and never will be. And if the Lord had not cut short the days, no human being would be saved. But for the sake of the elect, whom he chose, he shortened the days.

One question that arises when considering the Yeshua's statement is "From what time frame will those days be cut short?" Applying the knowledge of how God often uses numbers as presented previously in this book, if Yeshua should return before the Hebraic year of 6000, that would satisfy the criteria of having the days cut short. Likewise, if Yeshua should return prior to the 2000-year mark from His ascension in 30 AD, which is before 2030, that, too, would satisfy the criteria for having the days cut short. But could God also be applying His words to the final 7-year period? Independent of this specific prospect, does the final 7-year period have to be 7 *fully completed* years?

Many Bible scholars teach that the AOD will occur at the 3.5-year mark within the final 7-year period.

However, we know that from the time of the AOD there will be a fixed number of 1290 days until He returns. One thousand two hundred ninety days is 30 days longer than 3.5 years using the Hebraic 360 days per year. Therefore, this time is not precisely in the middle of a full 7-year period. Either the final 7-year period of Daniel's 70 weeks is slightly longer than a full 7 years or something else is being described. The NKJV states the AOD will occur in *the middle* of the week, and not precisely in the very center of the week.

DANIEL 9:27 (NKJV)
Then he shall confirm a covenant with many for one week; But in *the middle of the week* He shall bring an end to sacrifice and offering [Italics added]

If you look at a seven-candle menorah, the entire 4th candle is *the middle candle*. Likewise, with respect to a 7-year period, the *entire* 4th year is the middle year. Since God has stated there will be a fixed number of days in the *last part* of the 7-year period between the AOD and His return, looking back from the future, the only way the final 7-year period could be shortened would be for God to electively shorten *the first part* of the 7-year period. And for the AOD to remain *within* the 4th middle year, the maximum the first part of the 7-year period could be shortened or not fully completed would be one-day shy of 0.5 years. Of course, this is a speculative interpretation. This, too, will remain viable until proven otherwise by the passage of time.

CHAPTER 44

BRINGING THE NUMERICAL PUZZLE PIECES ALL TOGETHER – A HYPOTHETICAL MODEL

This hypothetical speculative model contains four major hypotheses. The first three hypotheses are based upon the aforementioned Biblically based numerical convergence on the Hebraic years of 5779–5780, which overlap the Gregorian years 2019–2020. They are also based upon the interpretation that God will electively use *two 7s* as seen in the middle of the Hebraic year 5779 as a numerical marker for the final 7-year season for His return. Ultimately, the timing of Yeshua's return *is exclusively His choice*. None of the first three hypotheses need be correct; these hypotheses will be proven valid or refuted within the next 7 years.

The model contains aspects that are *timed* hypotheses and others that are *non-timed* principles. The non-timed based principles *may continue to be valid* and *make contributions* to the understanding of future events, should the validity of the timed aspects of the model expire.

Please recall that I would not have bothered to write this book if I believed the information, as well as the means by which it was obtained, was totally random and had no merit to benefit others. *Parts I and II* of this book should remain a timeless benefit to readers. The potential benefit of the following hypothetical model is questionable at this time. After all, the model attempts to look into the future. At a minimum, perhaps the non-timed based principles contained in the model will be of merit. Ultimately, the passage of time will be the arbiter of which aspects of the hypothetical model will have merit and which will not.

INSTRUCTIONS ON HOW TO VIEW THE MODEL

This hypothetical model attempts to identify *time periods of high risk* based upon Divine Numerics and certain interpretations of Biblical Scripture. It does *not* predict when future events will happen. It is important that the reader understand the distinction between the above two statements. Going back to the hurricane analogy, there is a difference between saying that Florida is at a higher risk to be hit by a hurricane during the hurricane season and saying that I predict that a hurricane will hit Florida this hurricane season. One statement merely identifies a time period of high risk; whereas the other statement makes a prediction.

As we move through future time periods that this model identifies as high risk, if nothing of importance happens during these periods, the model is *not* wrong, as no predictions are being made. With non-event transitions through high risk periods, the model is functioning properly. And it will continue to do so until its expiration at the end of 2026. If nothing happens during a high risk period, we merely have made it through that identified period of high risk.

In the longer term perspective, the model identifies a 10-year period, 2016-2026, as *high risk* for WW III and higher probability for the return of Yeshua. The high risk period is based upon the seasons for war in the USA, Divine Numerics, and Biblical interpretations that may or may not be alternative perspectives from mainstream Biblical prophecy schools of thought. Within this 10-year period, three yearly periods of *very high risk* are identified. These are 2016, 2018-2020, and 2022-2023. These years are based upon the prophet Daniel's final seven-year period and upon the Biblical based numerical convergence on the Gregorian years 2019-2020 and on the Hebraic years 5779-5780. Finally, in the shortest term perspectives, the model identifies small pockets of *extremely high risk* within a given year. Most of these are based upon counting backwards by 1335 and 1290 days from future Jewish holidays of the years 2019-2020, 2022-2023, and 2026.

I plan to give additional insight and perspective on this model in a post book blog as we move through the identified high risk periods.

High Risk Time Window for WW III: 2016-2026

Very High Risk Time Year Periods: 2016, 2018-2020, 2022-2023

The following three hypothesis associate the very high risk years for WWIII with the potential return of Yeshua.

2016 - HYPOTHESIS #1: The Hebraic years 5779–5780 could mark the time of Yeshua's return at the Battle of Armageddon.

EXPIRATION: This hypothesis will be invalid if we successfully make it through the 2016-very high risk period for WWIII and the Abomination of Desolation (AOD) does not occur in 2016.

Two boundaries of time define the very high-risk period within the year 2016:

A. The earliest time of high risk is February 3–25, 2016 for the 1,335-day event of Daniel 12; followed by AOD 45 days later.

B. The latest time of high risk within 2016 is before October 10, 2016; followed by AOD 45 days later.

I will detail the extremely high risk smaller pockets of time within 2016, later in this chapter.

2018-2020 - HYPOTHESIS #2: The Hebraic years 5779–5780 could mark *the middle* of the final 7-year period.

EXPIRATION: This hypothesis will be invalid if we successfully make it through the 2018-2020 very high risk period for WWIII and the AOD does not occur in the Hebraic years 5779–5780 (September 2018–September 2020).

2022-2023 - HYPOTHESIS #3: The Hebraic years 5779–5780 could mark *the beginning* of the final 7-year period.

EXPIRATION: This hypothesis will be invalid if we successfully make it through the 2022-2023 very high risk period for WWIII and the AOD does not occur in the Hebraic years 5782–5783 (September 2021–September 2022).

HYPOTHESIS #4: None of the above is correct.

Let's examine the first two hypotheses in some detail.

2016 - HYPOTHESIS #1: The Hebraic years 5779–5780 could mark the time of Yeshua's return at the Battle of Armageddon.

In this hypothesis, 5779–5780 would mark the end of the final 7-year period. For this hypothesis to be correct, *several things must be true:*

1. The final 7-year period must have begun with a *non-public* agreement between the Antichrist and among leaders in the October 2012 to the June 6, 2013 time frame. This requirement

could have been fulfilled around the time of President Obama's Covenant of People's trip to Israel in 2013.

2. The general public will not know that the above agreement occurred until the *last moments* before the AOD occurs, at which time the Antichrist will stop daily sacrifices on the Temple Mount in Jerusalem.

3. Looking back from 2019–2020 by 1290 days, the AOD must occur in 2016.

4. Daily sacrifices of animals must occur on the Temple Mount in the year 2016 in order for the Antichrist to stop them.

5. The Antichrist need not have a physically rebuilt Jewish temple with a roof over his head to stop daily animal sacrifices on the Temple Mount.

6. The Antichrist does not have to physically sit in a chair in a rebuilt temple on the Temple Mount at the time of the AOD.

7. The last Biblical generation must be no longer than 1-day shy of 53 years and must have started on 6/7/1967. If

these two interpretations are true, then Yeshua must return prior to 6/6/2020. Looking back from the future, if we do not see the AOD in 2016, then either the start date of 6/7/1967 is wrong or a Biblical generation contains more than 52 full years. Perhaps then 60 years would be correct, as 6 x 10 = 60 and 6 is the number given to man. 6/7/1967 + 1-day shy of 61 years = 6/6/2028.

8. The *end* of the *13th cycle* of the living human Biblical end-time clock known as *Daf Yomi* will mark the season for the return of Yeshua.

9. The event associated with the 1,335 days of Daniel 12 must occur in 2016 and be an event that *precedes* the AOD event that occurs at 1,290 days before Yeshua's return.

10. The recent blood moon tetrad that occurred on four consecutive major Jewish holidays fell within the final 7-year time frame.

More discussion on Items 4 and 5:

Background information on Jewish temples on the Temple Mount area in Jerusalem

- The *First temple* was built by King Solomon in 957 BC. The Babylonians, under Nebuchadnezzar, destroyed this temple on the 9th of Av, 586 BC.

- The *Second temple*, the one that Yeshua walked and taught in, was built around 516 BC and later made extravagant by King Herod around 20 BC. The Romans destroyed this temple, also on the 9th of Av, but in the year 70 AD.

- The *Third temple* has not been constructed. No one knows at this time whether a fully completed *man-made* physical Temple will ever be built. If a third temple is rebuilt by man, then the temple referred to as *Ezekiel's Temple* would be the *fourth temple*. Both Ezekiel and Revelation 21 refer to Ezekiel's Temple.

The consideration of a third or fourth temple is not a new matter. According to Biblical scholar and author Roy A. Reinhold, "In 1993, there was a great controversy between the former Chief Sephardic Rabbi Mordechai Eliahu and Rabbi Yisrael Ariel who heads the Temple Institute, concerning whether it is the responsibility of Jews to build a third Temple or whether the Temple will be brought down from heaven when the Messiah comes."[24]

The Antichrist need not have a physical rebuilt Jewish temple with a roof over his head to stop daily animal sacrifices on the Temple Mount.

I have heard the assertion preached that the third temple will never be built because God's Holy Spirit will no longer inhabit buildings, but only inhabit the hearts of His believers. This assertion was based, in part, on the following:

1 CORINTHIANS 3: 16–17

Do you not know that you are God's temple and that God's Spirit dwells in you? [17] If anyone destroys God's temple, God will destroy him. For God's temple is holy, and you are that temple.

However, just because God's Spirit dwells in the hearts of His believers, this does not stop people, who do not acknowledge this, from *attempting* to rebuild the third temple, or to reinstitute animal sacrifice.

I originally thought that a physical rebuilt Jewish temple on the Temple Mount in Jerusalem had to be a reality in order for animal sacrifices to be started and stopped on the Temple Mount; and for the AOD to occur. However, as time passed, I realized that there wasn't enough time to complete construction on a Jewish temple prior to 2016.

My understanding regarding the requirement for a physical rebuilt Jewish temple changed by early 2015, when I received an email stating that the Temple Institute in Jerusalem had completed the construction of their sacrificial altar. This email led me to look more closely at the Temple Institute's website. The Temple Institute is the foremost organization leading the effort to re-establish Jewish temple worship on the Temple Mount in Jerusalem. *They say* on their website that they *do not need* to have a physically rebuilt Temple to restart animal sacrifices on the Temple Mount. They specifically say, "The divine service, including the offerings, can begin before the building of the temple itself, once the altar is built and standing in its proper place." They also say that they don't even need the ashes of a Red Heifer to restart animal sacrifices.[25] To emphasize, these are *their* words, not mine. As such, the possibility for animal sacrifice on the Temple Mount in Jerusalem without a physically rebuilt temple building remains a possibility, until proven otherwise.

The argument that the Antichrist need not have a physical rebuilt Jewish temple is also supported by Scripture.

REVELATION 11:1–2

Then I was given a measuring rod like a staff, and I was told, "Rise and ***measure the temple of God and the altar and those who worship there***, but do not measure the court outside the temple; leave that out, for it is given over to the nations, and they will trample the holy city for forty-two months. [Bold type and Italics added]

This Scripture says *measure the temple*; not measure *and build* the temple. Any building constructed today first has a set of blueprints. You can have the blueprints for a building, but the building does not have to be constructed. This occurs commonly.

Item 6:
The Antichrist does not have to physically sit in chair in a rebuilt temple on the Temple Mount at the time of the AOD.

It has been said to me that a physical rebuilt Temple had to be in place because Scripture says that the Antichrist will sit in the temple of God. Although this may end up being true, it doesn't *have to be true.* Let's examine this more closely.

2 THESSALONIANS 2:4 (CJB)

He will oppose himself to **everything** that people call a **god** or make an object of worship; **he will put himself above** them all, so that *he will sit* in the Temple **of God** and proclaim that he himself is **God**. [Some Bold and Italics added]

Will the Antichrist literally or figuratively sit in the temple of God? The examination of other Scriptures suggests that this "sitting" may be figurative: The Antichrist does not have to be *literally* sitting down in a physical chair with a rebuilt temple roof over his head.

In the Bible, the image of *sitting* is one synonymous with having authority. Being *seated on a throne* equals a *figurative* representation of authority. According to the Oxford Dictionary, a *throne* is a noun used to signify *sovereign power*: as in "the heir to the throne." Therefore, when we see Yeshua, who is referred to in the following passages, sitting on a throne, we see a reference to one who is *seated with sovereign authority*.

MARK 16:19 (CJB)
So then, after he had spoken to them, the Lord Yeshua was taken up into heaven and **sat at the right hand of God**.

REVELATION 7:15
Therefore, they are before the throne of God, and serve him day and night in his temple; and he who *sits on the throne* will shelter them with his presence. [Italics added]

This figurative imagery is seen also in the following.

EPHESIANS 2:5–6 (CJB)
it is by grace that you have been delivered. That is, God raised us up with the Messiah Yeshua and *seated us with him* in heaven, [Italics added]

Below, we see an association between power, authority and a throne given to the beast of Revelation 13 by the dragon, Satan.

REVELATION 13:2

And to it the dragon gave *his power* and *his throne* and *great authority*. [Bold type and Italics added]

Therefore, there exists much Scriptural evidence supporting the assertion that the Antichrist need not be literally sitting in a completed rebuilt third Jewish temple in order for animal sacrifices to be stopped. Also, a physically rebuilt temple, complete with a roof overhead, need not be in place for the Antichrist to be "standing in the holy place" as described in Matthew 24:15.

Additional puzzle pieces pertinent to Hypothesis #1

In order to fully appreciate the depth of information supporting Hypothesis #1, it is necessary for me to throw all the potential puzzle pieces on the table. So please bear with me. If any of the parts of this model turn out to be true, it is important for all of this information to have been written down beforehand in order to refute any allegations that the information was reported after the fact.

For Hypothesis #1 to be correct, the AOD must occur in 2016. Therefore, we need to consider other evidence that potentially supports the focus on 2016. All but one of the following points are also applicable to Hypothesis #2. None are applicable to Hypothesis #3.

In 2016, the world's population will reach 7.4 billion people.[26] Similar to the application of God's numbers

7/4 to the birth of the United States of America, this may also have an analogous implication. It may also represent the maximum population that this world will ever reach before massive destruction begins.

The day of the United States: 240 years

Also on 7/4/2016, America will be 240 years old. Similar to 24 hours in a day, 240 years potentially marks the numerical equivalent of the end of the day for the United States. Will 2016 also mark the *last* day for the USA? At our nation's founding, we embraced the freedom that came from God. The Declaration of Independence proclaimed that it was *specifically* God, who endowed all mankind with certain unalienable rights. Now, our society increasingly embraces a freedom *apart* from God.

As a corollary to the above, back in 2007, I said, "The next US president elected in 2008 will be the 44th president. The numbers are implying that this person will be a two-term President and will be the last President of the United States. I'll be very happy to be wrong, but I'm sticking to this until I see the 45th president sworn in." Under Hypothesis #1, there may *not* be an American election in November of 2016.

Also, in January 2016, the US federal debt will eclipse $19 Trillion.[27] The Bible gives many warnings against the folly of being excessively in debt. 19 is a numerical marker representing a final judgment by God. If correctly interpreted, this forebodes a massive financial collapse in 2016.

Please also recall from Chapter 3 of Part III that Larry Edelson's *secularly based* analysis of 3 different categories of cycles that all converge on 2016. These suggest financial turmoil and war in 2016.

Another cycle of pertinent Biblical numbers will occur in 2016. The Balfour Declaration, published in the press 11/9/1917 (72 years prior to the fall of the Berlin Wall on 11/9/1989), confirmed support from the British government for the establishment for a national home for the Jewish people in the territory then known as Palestine. This date in the Hebraic calendar was 5678, a numerical sequence. The Balfour Declaration marked a time of significant transition for the Jewish people. Using whole numbers, 7 x 7 (49) years later after the Balfour Declaration, the transition of 6/7/1967 occurred. The high significance of two 7s and the transition from 6 to 7 has already been discussed in this book. 7 x 7 (49) years added to the 6/7/1967 transition falls within the year 2016. Therefore, this yields the following cycle: 1917 + *49* = 1967 + *49* = 2016.

Finally, there are two additional anecdotal stories I need share with you.

First, my friend Dr. G, the orthodox Jewish gastroenterologist, decided he was going to send me a video on Torah codes.[28] I received the email link on May 20, 2015. Rabbi Matityahu Glazerson was being interviewed about his work with Torah codes and gematria. He has found numerous codes that point to the coming of Messiah in 776, which he asserts means the Hebraic year 5776. This is within 2016. Two out of the four major hypotheses in this chapter also focus on the link between 5776 and the return of Messiah, but these are derived from totally different methodologies than the rabbi's gematria. Even more shocking, at the 6:00 minute mark in the video, the Rabbi uses gematria to interpret the verse Daniel 12:11. He concludes that the 1,335-day event found in the verse has something to do with 2016.

Was this another fluke or orchestration? First of all, Dr. G had never before sent me any video. Second, the 1,335-day event is one that is fairly obscure and rarely talked about even in Biblical prophetic circles. Third, the rabbi had come up with the same conclusion that I had come up with using totally different numerical methodologies: the conclusion that the event of 1,335 days will be associated with the Hebraic year 5776! Only time will tell if this story is a fluke; one superimposed upon several other flukes that all focus on 2016.

A numerical corollary to this rabbi's finding potentially ties together the "776" of the Hebraic year 5776, to Rabbi Jonathan Cahn's discovery of the Isaiah 9:10 Judgment, and to the Freedom Tower in New York City. If the parallel Rabbi Cahn discovered continues to play out because America did not heed the warnings of God from 9/11, the next time New York City will be hit could be an event of greater devastation. In that potential future event, the *Freedom Tower* could also be totally destroyed. The Freedom Tower was built as a memorial to the victims of the fallen Twin Towers that fell during the 9/11 attack on New York City.

Numerically, the Freedom Tower is also marked with 776, as its height is *1,776* feet tall.

The second anecdotal story is as follows. In late July 2015, a book suggestion by Amazon caught my eye: *Antichrist 2016–2019: Mystery Babylon, Barack Obama & the Islamic Caliphate* by David Montaigne.[29] This author's timeline of 2016–2019 is consistent to Hypothesis #1 of this book. He also had made note of the possibility that, in early 2013, a secret agreement could have been made that started the final 7-year countdown. Along this line, he makes an excellent point based on the following Scripture:

LUKE 13:6–7, 9
THE PARABLE OF THE BARREN FIG TREE
And he told this parable: "A man had a fig tree planted in his vineyard, and he came seeking fruit on it and found none. And he said to the vinedresser, 'Look, *for three years* now I have come seeking fruit on this fig tree, and I find none. Cut it down. Then if it should bear fruit *next year*, well and good; but if not, you can cut it down.'" [Italics added]

Mr. Montaigne makes the point that after three years of seeing nothing happen, similar to seeing nothing happen in the first part of the final 7-year period, the impatient man would see his evidence in the *fourth year*.[29] This suggestion is also consistent with the interpretation presented in Part III, Chapter 42, regarding the very last moment warnings that Noah and Lot received.

Specific Hypothetical Speculative Model based upon 2016 - HYPOTHESIS #1: The Hebraic years 5779–5780 could mark the time of Yeshua's return at the Battle of Armageddon.

EXPIRATION: This hypothesis will be invalid if we successfully make it through the 2016 very high risk period for WWIII and the Abomination of Desolation (AOD) does not occur in 2016.

CAUTION: The *specific details* about potential events associated with this model are *highly speculative*. The *general* concepts contained within the model are more reasonably speculative. All interpretations lay within the Spectrum of Speculation that I have previously discussed. I, in no way, can see the future. At a minimum, some parts of the following model most likely will be wrong. The whole model could be wrong. If you have a disdain for travelling down a road of speculation to this degree, then I would suggest that you not read the following. If major world events do occur in the future along the lines discussed in this book, you could always read the following *after* the fact.

The Biblically based numerics presented in this book suggest 2016 is a year of very high risk for the world. The following speculation is based primarily from the perspective of *looking back from the future*. As we look forward into the future from the time this text is being written, the events of part A below seem *very improbable* to even the closest observers of the world events. However, if some of the following events do occur, I would be remiss if I didn't include them in this part of the hypothetical model. These events do, however, seem a bit more probable if we look backwards from the future, instead of looking forward into the future.

A. The first time pocket of extremely high risk is identified as February 3–25, 2016.

The timing of this timeframe is based upon looking back by 1335 days from the future of the Jewish fall feast period of 2019. *We may have already successfully made it through this period of by the time you read this.* If so, this is good! It means we have made it safely through an extremely high risk period. In this favorable outcome, keep in mind that the following hypothetical tenets and concepts presented below still could be applicable to any other *future* pockets of extremely high risk occurring within the next 10 year period.

In this speculative scenario, a massive financial crisis precedes World War III. Historically, significant wars often occur after a major financial crisis. When countries are busy making money, they usually put off their disagreements for another time. Take money away from them – and now they are ready to fight. Recall that the Great Depression of the 1930s created a dire worldwide economic environment. This was especially true in Germany. The extremely dire economic state in Germany in the 1930s created an environment in which Adolph Hitler and his Nazi party were able to rise and thrive, until their defeat.

Our future financial crisis could be initiated by numerous causes. Most likely, the US National debt will be a major contributing factor. I do not know the specific event that will be blamed for precipitating the crisis. In one scenario, with the price of oil being so low, Saudi Arabia could stop selling their oil in US dollars. The resultant *currency crisis* could have a massive domino effect in markets throughout the world. The US has had the luxury of printing as many dollars as the Federal Reserve wanted. If the US dollar is no longer considered the world reserve currency, the days of unlimited printing of money with unlimited impunity will be over. This could send a major shockwave throughout all the world's financial markets.

The financial crisis could occur as early as the very end of January 2016. Often by design, major financial crises are announced over a weekend when the financial markets are closed. We saw this occur with the Bear Sterns' announcement by the Federal Reserve in March 2008. If a similar announcement occurs over a weekend, we could see the Dow Jones Industrial Average open up Monday morning down by greater than 3,000 points.

I repeat this for emphasis: After nations loose massive wealth, they will be angry and ready to fight, especially if nations start pointing fingers at each other for causing the financial collapse. Noah had a 7-day warning before the Great Flood occurred. Perhaps, we could have *two 7s* or 14 days of warning between the financial collapse and the start of World War III (WWIII), since the return of Yeshua is strongly marked by two 7s.

World War III could kill over 2.4 billion people. This would be consistent with the sixth trumpet war, which is found in Revelation 9. In order to account for one-third of the world's population killed in the 6th trumpet war, you must include Asia. As such, this war most likely would be a nuclear war and include the nations of China, the United States of America and probably India and Pakistan.

Within days after 2.4 billion people are killed, the entire remaining world population will be in shock. Those in Israel will fully realize they must turn toward God. The Israelis immediately move to re-institute animal sacrifice on the Temple Mount in Jerusalem. The rest of the world is horrified by the scenes of sacrificing animals in a religious ceremony. This practice does not last very long. Within 45 days after the 1,335-day event of the massive nuclear strikes of WW III, the individual to be known as the Antichrist will stop the animal sacrifices on the Temple Mount as the AOD unfolds. The final 1,290-day countdown to the return of Yeshua begins. The restraint of God's Holy Spirit upon all people not reborn with His Spirit will be lifted and the Great Tribulation of ungodly, horrid, lawless behavior will begin.

B. The second time pocket of extremely high risk is identified as April 27 through May 4, 2016.

The timing of this timeframe is based upon looking back by 1335 days from the future *of Chanukah 2019*. Arguments for supporting this time frame are made by David Montaigne.[29] The reality that Yeshua is the light of the world and that Chanukah is the festival of lights are supportive of this interpretation. Again, it is possible that we may have already successfully made it through this period of by the time you read this.

C. The third time pocket of extremely high risk is identified as August 8-12, 2016.

The timing of this timeframe is based upon looking back from the future *of Nisan 10-14, 5780*, in the Hebraic calendar, (April 4-8, 2020). This timeframe is particularly interesting, both theologically and numerically.

Theologically, this time frame represents an alternative perspective to what Jewish holiday best matches the time of Yeshua's future return: The Jewish Fall Feast period. Please recall the symbolic analogy I have previously written about regarding the return of Yeshua. Yeshua will return after the last trumpet blast. Yom Kippur ends with a long trumpet blast. The Jubilee year begins after a long trumpet blast. And God brought down the walls of Jericho after the long trumpet blast and numerically marked this event with two 7s. All of these events point to a return of Yeshua within an 11- to 12-day window of time between the end of Yom Kippur and the end of a Jewish fall feast of some future year.

However, God may use the above symbolic analogy more as a marker of the beginning of a *season* leading to His return rather than an exact time marker. The reason for this may be that God cares more about giving *absolute maximum time* possible for all who will repent to do so, compared to making the Jewish Fall Feast symbolic analogy fit perfectly within our earthly timeline.

I recently attended a prophetic conference given by Dr. Irvin Baxter. For some reason, three words in a Scripture he quoted really struck me in my spirit: *no more delay*.

REVELATION 10:5-7

And the angel whom I saw ... swore by him who lives forever and ever, ... that there would be *no more delay*, but that in the days of the trumpet call to be sounded by the *seventh* angel, the mystery of God would be fulfilled... [Bold type and Italics added]

In what way is the seventh and last trumpet *delayed*? One might expect that the seventh angel would blow the seventh trumpet immediately after Yom Kippur. But is it possible that this will be delayed from Yom Kippur of some future year to give humanity more time to repent?

If delayed, the next question that logically follows is, "Delayed until what other event or time marker?" The Nisan 10-14, 5780 time frame is presented in this model as an interesting alternative possible answer to this question. Biblically at the time of Yeshua's coming, during this time frame Jewish families would start to inspect their Passover lamb for imperfections on Nisan 10. It was during this very same calendar time frame that the people of Jerusalem failed to recognize the truth that Yeshua was the Lamb of God: the authorities rejected and crucified Him. On Nisan 10, the following occurred.

LUKE 19:41-44
JESUS WEEPS OVER JERUSALEM
And when he [Yeshua] drew near and saw the city, he wept over it, saying, "Would that you, even you, had known on this day the things that make for peace! But now they are hidden from your eyes. For the days will come upon you, when your enemies will set up a barricade around you and surround you and hem you in on every side and tear you down to the ground, you and your children within you. And they will not leave one stone upon another in you, *because you did not know the time of your visitation*." [Bold type and Italics added]

Theologically, the *second* time Yeshua presents Himself to the people of Jerusalem for inspection, He will be recognized. Will the following happen on Nisan 10 of some future year?

ZECHARIAH 12:10
HIM WHOM THEY HAVE PIERCED
"And I will pour out on the house of David and the inhabitants of Jerusalem a spirit of grace and pleas for mercy, so that, *when they look on me, on him whom they have pierced*, they shall mourn for him, as one mourns for an only child,

and weep bitterly over him, as one weeps over a
firstborn. [Bold type and Italics added]

Also, theologically interesting is that on one hand
Yeshua's return is *hastened*. This is described in Part III,
Chapter 43.

MARK 13:20
And if the Lord had not *cut short the days, no
human being would be saved*. But for the sake
of the elect, whom he chose, he shortened the
days. [Bold type and Italics added]

On the other hand, the seventh trumpet may be
delayed as described above. So a potential dynamic
timing give-and-take may be operative.

Nisan 10-14, 5780 is also *numerically* interesting.
First of all, President Obama landed in Israel on Nisan
10 in the year 2013 to begin his Covenant of Peoples
trip. Seven years from this date takes us to Nisan 10
in the year 2020. Second, Nisan 10 in 2020 is also
4/4/2020. This is a double numerical repeating pattern
that is also rich for Divine numerical interpretation. In
fact, counting backwards from the future 4/4/2020 by
1335 days yields a variant of another double numerical
repeating pattern: 8/8/2016.

**D. The forth and *latest* time pocket of extremely
high risk within 2016 is identified as before October
10, 2016; followed by AOD 45 days later.**

This period is based upon a correct interpretation of what quantitatively defines a Biblical generation. If you count backwards exactly 1,335 days from 6/6/2020, which is the last potential day for a full 52-year Biblical generation that starts on 6/7/67, then you arrive on the day October 10, 2016. This date is within the Jewish Fall Feast of 2016. 45 days after this date is November 24, 2016, which would be the 1,290th day that marks the AOD. This is also Thanksgiving Day, 2016. Please note that 6/6/2020 is also a double numerical repeating pattern.

If the AOD does not occur prior to November 24, 2016, then a Biblical generation is not 52 years long and / or the starting date of this Biblical generation of 6/7/67 is incorrect. Also, if the AOD does not occur prior to this date, then the strong covenant referred to in Daniel 9:27 was not among the secret, non-public agreements made at the time of President Obama's March 21, 2013 trip to Israel, which was code named *A Covenant of Peoples*. The numerical transitional markers of the 67th year of operation for the UN and the 12 to 13 transitional pattern seen within 2012-2013 will also be invalid numerical markers of the final 7-year period. Also the long count of the Mayan Calendar of 13.0.0.0.0 and the start of the 13th cycle of Daf Yomi will not be markers for the beginning of the final 7-year season.

If the AOD does not occur before the November 16, 2016, then Rabbi Matityahu Glazerson's gematria linkage of Daniel's 1,335-day event to the Hebraic year 5776 will be invalidated. Counting backward 45 days from this day yields the last day of 5776, October 2, 2016. If true, then my anecdotal story about the rabbi's gematria will be a fluke.

If for some reason Rabbi Glazerson's gematria is valid to the last day of 2016, and if the AOD does not occur on or before February 14, *2017* (Valentine's Day 2017), then gematria linkage of Daniel's 1,335-day event to 2016 will be also invalidated. Counting backwards 45 days from Valentine's Day 2017 yields the last day of 2016, December 31, 2016.

2018-2020 - HYPOTHESIS #2: The Hebraic years 5779–5780 could mark *the middle* of the final 7-year period.

This hypothesis would shift *the beginning* of the last 7-year period to the year 2016. Within this hypothesis, the methodology of looking back from the future remains a valid approach until disproven. In addition, the following could still be associated possibilities. If the 1,335-day event of Daniel is not WW III, and if instead WW III marks *the beginning* of the final 7-year period and occurs in the year 2016, then the 240-year history of the USA could still mark the end of the day for the country. The 44th US president could still be the last president elected. The $19 trillion US national debt still could represent a symbolic marker with 19 representing God's final judgment in divine order. The world population reaching 7.4 billion people in 2016 still could be a numerical marker associated with the final 7-year period. Other components of Hypothesis #1 may or may not be applicable.

Under this hypothesis, the blood moon tetrad of 2014–2015 would *not* fall within the final 7-year season. However, it still could be an astronomical precursor of this final period.

2022-2023 - HYPOTHESIS #3: The Hebraic years 5779–5780 could mark *the beginning* of the final 7-year period.

This hypothesis would shift *the beginning* of the last 7-year period to the years 2019–2020. The Biblically based numbers presented in this book converge on these years. Within this hypothesis, the methodology of looking back from the future years of 2026–2027 remains a valid approach until disproven. In addition, the following could still be associated possibilities. WW III could still occur within the 10-year period suggested by the seasons for war: 2016–2026. Yeshua would still return earlier than the 2,000-year mark from His ascension in 30 AD. The last Biblical generation could still have started on 6/7/67, but the length of this generation could be based upon a multiple of the number given to man: 60 years, instead of 52 years. Also, under this hypothesis, the *end* of the 13th cycle of Daf Yomi could still mark the *beginning* of the final 7-year period.

Assessment of Probabilities associated with Hypotheses # 1 through # 3

At this time, there are more numerical pieces that support Hypothesis # 1 (AOD in 2016) than

Hypotheses #2 and #3. However, this reality may be biased by the fact that we are closer in time to the events described in Hypothesis #1. All speculation aside, until we see the AOD occur, only God knows when He will elect to return.

Rapture timing by the numbers

At some time within the final 7-year period, true believers in Yeshua will be taken out of our 4th-dimensional earth realm by God into the heavenly dimensions. These other dimensions lie within the additional 6 dimensions proven to exist by particle physicists in the String and M Theories (see also Part I, Chapter 8). There are several different interpretations that deal with when this rapture will occur in relationship to the final 7-year period. All arguments have excellent Biblical support. *But if God's numbers could vote on the question, what timing would they favor?*

First of all, I will remind everyone that those who are raptured out of the earth realm could enter a totally independent time line. Those raptured could spend an equivalent of 7 full years in the heavenly time realm and still return to the earth realm within 1 second of when they left! In this light, it is possible that the rapture occurs at the very last moments prior to the return of Yeshua. As such, rapture timing theories based upon spending a full 7 years preparing for the wedding feast with Yeshua could still occur on a time clock in the heavenly realm, yet not necessarily on the time clock of the earth realm. The earth and heavenly time clocks should not be confused or conflated. They could be totally independent from each other.

Here is one Scripture referring to the rapture:

1 CORINTHIANS 15:51-53
Behold! I tell you a mystery. We shall not all sleep, but we shall all be changed, in a moment, in the twinkling of an eye, ***at the last trumpet***. For the trumpet will sound, and the dead will be raised imperishable, and we shall be changed. For this perishable body must put on the imperishable, and this mortal body must put on immortality. [Bold type and Italics added]

There are a total of 7 trumpets. Therefore, the last trumpet is the 7th trumpet. The 6th trumpet is the war that kills one-third of mankind. If this war is WW III, then the rapture will occur after WW III. The time *between* the 6th and 7th trumpets numerically symbolize the transition from man to God. This is consistent with how God uses numbers. *This is how the numbers would vote, if they could.*

Along the numerical line of a 6th to 7th transition pattern, it is also possible that the rapture will occur during the 6th year out of the final 7-year period. If Yeshua chooses to return in 2019, then the 6th year could be 2018. 18 is the number for eternal life. 19 is the number for a final judgment. All numerical interpretation aside, the precise timing of the rapture will most likely remain a mystery until it actually happens.

The most important contribution that I can make to theories about this topic is to remind all that *the timelines of the earth and heavenly realms may be independent* of each other. We should attempt to think outside of our 4th-dimensional bubble.

Conclusion about the hypothetical speculative model

Because no human can see the future with 100 percent accuracy, the model presented in this chapter will remain speculative until proven either valid or invalid. However, because this model is based upon numerous and substantial pieces of evidence, a reasonable probability exists that *some* components presented of the model may fall closer to the more probable end of the spectrum of speculation.

The model contains aspects that are *timed* hypotheses and others that are *non-timed* principles. The timed aspects do have an expiration period to their validity. This expiration period spans from as early as February 2016 for some hypotheses to the absolute latest time, which is sometime in 2026 or 2027. The timed aspects of the model are *not predictions*. Rather, the model seeks to identify *high risk periods of time*. If a high risk period of time passes without an important event occurring, we merely have made it through that identified high risk period and the timed based aspect of the model continues to function as expected until the time of its expiration.

The non-timed-based principles *may continue to be valid* and *make contributions* to the understanding of future events, should the validity of the timed aspects of the model expire. Therefore, these aspects of the model could make a timeless contribution to prophetic understanding.

I have laid out on the table all the puzzle pieces that I have been exposed to over the past 12 to 13 years. As we move together into the future, we will know whether they will be significant or not.

If none of the speculative models presented in this chapter turn out to be correct, this book still should make a contribution to society. The information presented in Part II still should act as a reference for people reading the Bible to gain a deeper level of understanding from the contributions that the numbers make to the Biblical text. Information found in Part I may also continue to make contributions to Biblical understanding.

CHAPTER 45

THE NUMBER "FEW": A VERY UNPOPULAR MESSAGE TO THE MAJORITY OF THE WORLD

I have been showing the seasons for war in the United States of America to people since 2003. I have shown many people other numerical evidences of things likely to come in our lifetime. After I do so, one of the most common responses I hear is, "Wow! Those numbers are really scary!"

Having lived with this numerical knowledge for 12 to 13 years now, I have had the opportunity to gain a longer-term perspective of what may happen in the near future. So when people say to me, "Wow! Those numbers are really scary!" I respond, "These numbers do not concern me much, especially in light of the number 'few'. For me, that's potentially the scariest number in the entire Bible!" People then say, "What do you mean by the number 'few'?" I respond, "You know, God gave us thousands upon thousands of numbers in the Bible. And He gave us hundreds, if not thousands, of hidden numerical clues about the future and about deeper meanings of Scripture. However, He has also chosen to be *non-specific* concerning the number many consider to be the most important! That number is: How many people will make it to heaven and avoid hell?"

God Almighty has chosen to tell us that the number is *FEW*. Being a numbers person, I say, "Few? This is concerning! What does that mean? 49 percent? 8.0 percent? 2.0 percent? .02 percent?" In one Scripture, *few* is linked to 8, the number for *a new beginning that lasts for all eternity*. This definition could fit the circumstance of an eternal salvation, but it is still a frightfully small number.

1 PETER 3:20–22 (CJB)
God waited patiently during the building of the ark, in which *a few people* — to be specific, *eight*— were delivered by means of water. [Bold type and Italics added]

It appears likely that even many people, who attend Christian churches and believe that they will be "OK" just because they attend church, may be eternally shocked at the day of their personal judgment. Please consider the following:

I NEVER KNEW YOU
Not everyone who says to me, 'Lord, Lord,' will enter the kingdom of heaven, but the one who does the will of my Father who is in heaven. On that day *many* will say to me, 'Lord, Lord, did we not prophesy in your name, and cast out

demons in your name, and do many mighty works in your name?' And then will I declare to them, *'I never knew you; depart from me, you workers of lawlessness.* [Bold type and Italics added]

MATTHEW 7:13–14

Enter by the narrow gate. For the gate is wide and the way is easy that leads to destruction, and those who enter by it *are many*. For the gate is narrow and the way is *hard that leads to life*, and those who find it are *few*. [Bold type and Italics added]

LUKE 13:22–28
THE NARROW DOOR

He went on his way through towns and villages, teaching and journeying toward Jerusalem. And someone said to him, **"Lord, will those who are saved be** *few***?"** And he said to them, "Strive to enter through the narrow door. **For *many*, I tell you, will seek to enter and will not be able.** When once the master of the house has risen **and shut the door**, and you begin to stand outside and to knock at the door, saying, 'Lord, open to us,' then he will answer you, 'I do not know where you come from.' Then you will begin to say, 'We ate and drank in your presence, and you taught in our streets.' But he will say, 'I tell you, I do not know where you come from. **Depart from me, all you workers of evil!'** In

that place there will be weeping and gnashing of teeth [Bold type and Italics added]

In light of *all you now know* after reading this book about how God uses numbers so specifically, consistently and amazingly, why do you think He has chosen to tell us that the number of people who will be entering heaven is *"FEW"*? Even though the invitation for the free gift of salvation and Eternal Life is open to all, *few* end up choosing what God has deemed is the only narrow gate or door through which we may pass. *Yeshua is that door!*

JOHN 10:7–9

So Jesus again said to them, "Truly, truly, I say to you, **I am the door** of the sheep. All who came before me are thieves and robbers, but the sheep did not listen to them. **I am the door**. If anyone enters by me, *he will be saved* [Bold type and Italics added]

JOHN 14:6

Yeshua said, "**I AM the Way — and the Truth and the Life**; *no one comes to the Father except through me.* [Bold type and Italics added]

Because God is outside of time, He already knows who has chosen or will choose the narrow gate or door to heaven and eternal life with Him. And He already knows that the number will be *FEW*. It's a done deal.

This is scary! Yeshua is the only door to heaven – no one will enter heaven except through Him. He created the universe and He gets to write the rules, not us. What will you do before His door is shut? Salvation is a matter of *heart first, brain second*. Will you open your heart to Him? Do this immediately, before His door is permanently shut. If this happens, He did not reject you; *you have rejected Him*. He loves you and He is waiting for you at His door. He is a God of love and also a God of order. You must accept Him as *both* Savior and *Lord* of your life.

APPENDIX:

QUICK REFERENCE GUIDE TO HOW GOD USES NUMBERS

The following are according to the explanations presented in this book.

The number 1. There is only *one* God. We need to put Him *first* in everything we do.

The number 7 represents *a completed act of perfection by God in the earth realm.*

The number 6 is the number *given to man by God* and / or *to the imperfect efforts of man.* In our material earth realm, man's efforts, represented by 6, *fall short* of God's perfection, represented by "7".

The number 3. When God completes an act in the *spirit* realm, it is most often associated with the number 3. Note that God uses *both* number 3 and number 7 as numbers of *completion*. The difference between these two numbers is defined by *where* the act was completed: heaven or earth.

The number 4. God commonly uses the number 4 to symbolize *the earth realm*. He also uses it to describe something that *starts* in one place on the *earth* and then eventually *spreads* or *expands full circle* around the earth or to the *four corners* of the earth.

The number 40. God uses the number 40 to represent *a time of trial and/or testing that leads to a new birth or a new beginning*. New beginnings associated with the number 40 start new eras, which do not last forever. They end with the start of yet another new era. In this respect, new beginnings associated with the number 40 are often *cyclical* in nature.

The number 8. God also uses the number 8 to symbolize *a new beginning*. Therefore, *both* numbers 8 and 40 contain meanings of a new beginning. However, unlike the new beginning associated with the number 40 that has an endpoint, a new beginning associated with the number 8 is one *that will last for all eternity*. There will be no subsequent new beginning to follow.

The number 5 is the number of *God's Grace*. We are saved by grace alone through the Father's gift of Yeshua, whose base number is 2, followed by the gift of His Holy Spirit, 3, entering our hearts. This is symbolized in the simple mathematical equation: $2 + 3 = 5$.

The number 10 is associated with *God's divine order*.

The number 12 is God's number for *wise counsel and / or divine government*.

The number 11. When *a group of people* get together and do something that is *unwise in God's eyes*, a number 11 is often associated with it. 11 *falls short* of God's number for wise counsel, divine government, the number 12.

The number 13 is God's number for *His priests and for His priestly nations.*

The number 18 is used by God to represent *eternal life.* 8 + 10 = 18.

The number 9. God most often uses the number 9 to represent *a judgment.* The verdict or outcome of a judgment can take the form of a blessing or of a curse. If the judgment is in the form of a curse, 9 can be associated with chaos and destruction. If the judgment is in the form of a blessing, 9 can be associated with the fruits and gifts of God's Holy Spirit. The chaos and destruction associated with 9 *falls short* of God's divine order, 10.

The number 19. In a similar numerical format to the number 18, 8 + 10 = 18, God may be using the number 19, 9 + 10 = 19, to represent or foreshadow *the FINAL judgment of all humanity.*

The transitional pattern of 6 to 7: God uses 6 to 7 as a numerical pattern to mark a *transition* between the imperfect works and efforts of man, 6, and the completion of a perfect act of God in the earth realm, 7. It also marks *a spiritual transition from man to God.*

The number 2. Yeshua's *base* number is the number 2. God uses multiple second-choice patterns in the First Testament to foreshadow Christ as the Second Adam. He is the second manifestation of the Godhead. He always has at least two witnesses. He will physically return to the earth realm in His Second Coming. The Second Testament is all about Yeshua.

Two 7s numerically represent the Word of God. This also represents a completed act of God in the earth realm *specifically related to Yeshua*, whose base number is 2. Used as a numerical marker, two 7s must come first *before* Yeshua returns. In this light, two 7s numerically symbolize and foreshadow Yeshua's return at the last Battle of Armageddon.

ENDNOTES

1   Booker, Richard, *Torah: Law or Grace?* (Sounds of the Trumpet, Inc.) 2001.
2   http://www.goodreads.com/quotes/728509-the-depravity-of-man-is-at-once-the-most-empirically
3   http://aletheia-seekers.blogspot.com/2014_06_01_archive.html
4   http://www.pbs.org/wgbh/nova/physics/elegant-universe.html#elegant-universe
5   From the *Talmud Yerushalmi (Eruvin 3:9)*, http://www.chabad.org/holidays/JewishNewYear/template_cdo/aid/4381/jewish/Two-Days-of-Rosh-Hashanah.htm
6   http://www.geohive.com/earth/his_history3.aspx
7   Walid Shoebat, 2007 International Prophecy Conference, God's News Behind the News, www.godsnews.com
8   https://en.wikipedia.org/wiki/Apple_I
9   http://archive.gulfnews.com/indepth/irancrisis/Talks/10082053.html
10 http://www.jewfaq.org/barmitz.htm
11 http://superstore.wnd.com/The-Isaiah-910-Judgment-Is-There-An-Ancient-Mystery-That-Fortells-Americas-Future-DVD
12 http://www.landofthebrave.info/henry-hudson-facts.htm
13 https://www.barna.org/barna-update/culture/664-the-state-of-the-bible-6-trends-for-2014#.VJRquC5AA, Research Releases in Culture & Media, April 8, 2014
14 http://www.greatseal.com/committees/firstcomm/
15. http://www.templeinstitute.org/vessels_gallery_11.htm
16. Cutshall, Bryan, *Unlocking the Prophecy Code, Understanding Bible Mysteries in Types and Shadows*, (Pathway Press, 2005), Chapter 3: The Good Samaritan, 39-57.

---

17. https://www.christiancourier.com/articles/1155-myth-or-history-did-jerichos-walls-come-down
18. http://www.israel-a-history-of.com/walls-of-jericho.html
19. http://www.hebrew4christians.com/Holidays/Spring_Holidays/First_Fruits/first_fruits.html
20. http://www.hebrew4christians.com/Grammar/Unit_One/Aleph-Bet/Zayin/zayin.html
21. http://www.crossroad.to/articles2/04/teichrib-blending-gods.htm
22. http://www.endtime.com/podcast/coming-one-world-religion-1/
23. http://www.globalpost.com/dispatch/news/regions/middle-east/israel-and-palestine/130218/obamas-visit-israel-gets-official-logo
24. http://ad2004.com/prophecytruths/Articles/Prophecy/temple.html
25. https://www.templeinstitute.org/frequently-asked-questions.htm
26. http://www.geohive.com/earth/his_history3.aspx
27. http://www.usgovernmentspending.com/federal_debt
28. Torah codes evidence about messiah return in 2016, https://www.youtube.com/watch?v=c_DtqTcmB5E
29. David Montaigne, Antichrist 2016-2019: Mystery Babylon, Barack Obama & the Islamic Caliphate, (Create Space Independent Publishing Platform 2014), 118.

CPSIA information can be obtained
at www.ICGtesting.com
Printed in the USA
LVHW010448051020
667928LV00001B/36